CliffsNotes

Homer's
The Odyssey

By Stanley P. Baldwin, M.A.

IN THIS BOOK

- ■ Learn about the Life and Background of the Author
- ■ Preview an Introduction to the Epic
- ■ Study a graphical Character Map
- ■ Explore themes and literary devices in the Critical Commentaries
- ■ Examine in-depth Character Analyses
- ■ Reinforce what you learn with CliffsNotes Review
- ■ Find additional information to further your study in CliffsNotes Resource Center and online at www.cliffsnotes.com

IDG Books Worldwide, Inc.
An International Data Group Company
Foster City, CA • Chicago, IL • Indianapolis, IN • New York, NY

About the Author

Stanley P. Baldwin is a writer and teacher living in Nebraska.

Publisher's Acknowledgments

Editorial

Project Editor: Tracy Barr

Acquisitions Editor: Greg Tubach

Glossary Editors: The editors and staff of Webster's New World Dictionaries

Editorial Assistant: Michelle Hacker

Production

Indexer: York Production Services, Inc.

Proofreader: York Production Services, Inc.

IDG Books Indianapolis Production Department

CliffsNotes Homer's *The Odyssey*

Published by
IDG Books Worldwide, Inc.
An International Data Group Company
919 E. Hillsdale Blvd.
Suite 400
Foster City, CA 94404

www.idgbooks.com (IDG Books Worldwide Web site)

www.cliffsnotes.com (CliffsNotes Web site)

Printed in the United States of America

10 9 8 7 6 5 4 3 2 1

1O/RS/QV/QQ/IN

Distributed in the United States by IDG Books Worldwide, Inc.

Note: If you purchased this book without a cover, you should be aware that this book is stolen property. It was reported as "unsold and destroyed" to the publisher, and neither the author nor the publisher has received any payment for this "stripped book."

Library of Congress Cataloging-in-Publication Data

Baldwin, Stanley P.
  CliffsNotes Homer's The Odyssey / Stanley Baldwin.
    p. cm.
  Includes biographical references and index.
  ISBN 0-7645-8599-1 (alk. paper)
  1. Homer. Odyssey--Examinations--Study guides. 2. Odysseus (Greek mythology) in literature--Examinations--Study guides. 3. Epic poetry, Greek--Examinations--Study guides. I. Title: Homer's The Odyssey. II. Title.
PA4167 .B25 2000
883'.01--dc21   00--035076
                                                              CIP

Distributed by CDG Books Canada Inc. for Canada; by Transworld Publishers Limited in the United Kingdom; by IDG Norge Books for Norway; by IDG Sweden Books for Sweden; by IDG Books Australia Publishing Corporation Pty. Ltd. for Australia and New Zealand; by TransQuest Publishers Pte Ltd. for Singapore, Malaysia, Thailand, Indonesia, and Hong Kong; by Gotop Information Inc. for Taiwan; by ICG Muse, Inc. for Japan; by Intersoft for South Africa; by Eyrolles for France; by International Thomson Publishing for Germany, Austria and Switzerland; by Distribuidora Cuspide for Argentina; by LR International for Brazil; by Galileo Libros for Chile; by Ediciones ZETA S.C.R. Ltda. for Peru; by WS Computer Publishing Corporation, Inc., for the Philippines; by Contemporanea de Ediciones for Venezuela; by Express Computer Distributors for the Caribbean and West Indies; by Micronesia Media Distributor, Inc. for Micronesia; by Chips Computadoras S.A. de C.V. for Mexico; by Editorial Norma de Panama S.A. for Panama; by American Bookshops for Finland.

For general information on IDG Books Worldwide's books in the U.S., please call our Consumer Customer Service department at 800-762-2974.

For reseller information, including discounts and premium sales, please call our Reseller Customer Service department at 800-434-3422.

For information on where to purchase IDG Books Worldwide's books outside the U.S., please contact our International Sales department at 317-596-5530 or fax 317-572-4002.

For consumer information on foreign language translations, please contact our Customer Service department at 1-800-434-3422, fax 317-572-4002, or e-mail rights@idgbooks.com

For information on licensing foreign or domestic rights, please phone +1-650-653-7098.

For sales inquiries and special prices for bulk quantities, please contact our Order Services department at 800-434-3422 or write to the address above.

For information on using IDG Books Worldwide's books in the classroom or for ordering examination copies, please contact our Educational Sales department at 800-434-2086 or fax 317-572-4005.

For press review copies, author interviews, or other publicity information, please contact our Public Relations department at 650-653-7000 or fax 650-653-7500.

For authorization to photocopy items for corporate, personal, or educational use, please contact Copyright Clearance Center, 222 Rosewood Drive, Danvers, MA 01923, or fax 978-750-4470.

Table of Contents

How to Use This Book

CliffsNotes The Odyssey supplements the original work, giving you background information about the author, an introduction to the poem, a graphical character map, critical commentaries, expanded glossaries, and a comprehensive index. CliffsNotes Review tests your comprehension of the original text and reinforces learning with questions and answers, practice projects, and more. For further information on Homer and The Odyssey, check out the CliffsNotes Resource Center.

CliffsNotes provides the following icons to highlight essential elements of particular interest:

Reveals the underlying themes in the work.

Helps you to more easily relate to or discover the depth of a character.

Uncovers elements such as setting, atmosphere, mystery, passion, violence, irony, symbolism, tragedy, foreshadowing, and satire.

Enables you to appreciate the nuances of words and phrases.

Don't Miss Our Web Site

Discover classic literature as well as modern-day treasures by visiting the Cliffs-Notes Web site at www.cliffsnotes.com. You can obtain a quick download of a CliffsNotes title, purchase a title in print form, browse our catalog, or view online samples.

You'll also find interactive tools that are fun and informative, links to interesting Web sites, tips, articles, and additional resources to help you, not only for literature, but for test prep, finance, careers, computers, and Internet, too. See you at www.cliffsnotes.com!

LIFE AND BACKGROUND OF THE AUTHOR

The Author

After well over 2,500 years, we still cannot say for sure who created the *Odyssey,* exactly how it was composed, or precisely when it was written. Even though there is little autobiographical information in the epic and not much else to go on, we can make some educated guesses based upon research by top scholars.

Most early Greeks had no doubt that there once was a single individual named Homer to whom they attributed authorship of *The Iliad, The Odyssey,* and the "Homeric Hymns," poems celebrating the ancient Greek gods. Although some seven different cities claimed to have been his birthplace, many thought Homer might have come from the island of Chios off the western coast of Asia Minor. In ancient times, a family bearing his name and living there was said to consist of his descendants.

Furthermore, because Homer composed his works in a form that blended Ionic and Aeolic dialects, it *is* likely that he was a native or resident of the western part of Asia Minor. He probably was a bard or rhapsode (a specialist in performing epics). Tradition has it that he was blind, a theory based largely on his portrayal of Demodocus, the blind singer of the Phaeacians (8.51), a passage in the "Hymns," and the somewhat romantic notion (partly supported by fact) that many such performers were blind.

The Homeric Question

By the second century BC, editors of the epics had raised what we now call the "Homeric Question." At issue are the authorship, origin, and means of composition of the works. Differences were noted in the styles and language of *The Iliad* and *The Odyssey.* Over the years, some critics have complained that the subjects and themes are too diverse for a single author. Some scholars even suggest that the works were the creation of a group. The dispute continues today.

In the past century, however, the preponderance of opinions seems to be on the side of single authorship. Some defend single authorship by citing William Shakespeare's varying approaches to *King Lear* and *The Tempest,* which deal with fading kings but in contrasting ways. Others point out that *The Iliad* appears to have been composed first and demonstrates the work of a younger man while the *Odyssey* is more mature and reflects an older author. Still others cite folk influences and the various themes and content as justification of conflicting styles.

During the late 1920s and early 1930s, an American scholar named Milman Parry revolutionized classical studies by demonstrating conclusively that both *The Iliad* and the *Odyssey* were composed in an oral, formulaic style based on tradition and designed to help the rhapsode perform a long piece from memory. The poems were recited, or more likely sung, to audiences in the way that similar works are presented in the *Odyssey*. The performer often accompanied himself with a lyre. Metrical phrases were used as mnemonic devices, and everyday language was altered to fit this poetic language. That would account for the "elevated style" that has long been attributed to the works.

Parry's discovery clearly alters how readers look at the authorship of the epics. Some scholars, like Harold Bloom (*Homer's Odyssey*, 1996, p. 8) think that Homer, if he existed, was no more than an editor or organizer of poems created by others, perhaps over generations. Others, such as Seth L. Schein (*Reading the Odyssey*, 1996, p. 4 ff.), credit the poet with considerable creativity while welcoming the evidence of oral tradition. Schein points out that Greeks apparently had access to the Phoenician alphabet by the third quarter of the eighth century BC and that a poet trained in the oral tradition could have written down (or dictated to a scribe) *The Odyssey* as readers now know it. He sees literary (written), as well as folk or traditional influences, in the creation of the epic.

Date of Composition

Although some scholars still maintain that the epic was written in its present form in the sixth century BC in Athens, mounting evidence indicates an earlier date. The weight of the scholarship implies that *The Odyssey* was probably composed and possibly written down about 700 BC. The most convincing argument is that *The Iliad* was written first. Both epics probably were created, in the form we know them, by the same poet—a theory that is consistent with the views of those who see unusual genius, as well as technical similarities, in each work. While this poet may have composed each work completely, he probably borrowed metrical phrases and content from other bards. These elements, after all, were the rhapsodes' tools in the oral tradition, belonging to all. Although relying significantly on folk tradition and devices of oral creativity, the version of *The Odyssey* that we now have seems to have been influenced most strongly by a single poet, probably a veteran rhapsode, who likely dictated it to a scribe or wrote it down himself.

Let's call him Homer.

INTRODUCTION
TO *THE ODYSSEY*

Introduction

An epic is a long narrative poem in an elevated style that deals with the trials and achievements of a great hero or heroes. The epic celebrates virtues of national, military, religious, political, or historical significance. The word "epic" itself comes from the Greek *épos*, originally meaning "word" but later "oration" or "song." Like all art, an epic may grow out of a limited context but achieves greatness in relation to its universality. It typically emphasizes heroic action as well as the struggle between the hero's ethos and his human failings or mortality.

Increasingly, scholars distinguish between two types of epic. The first, the *primary epic,* evolves from the mores, legends, or folk tales of a people and is initially developed in an *oral tradition* of storytelling. *Secondary epics*, on the other hand, are literary. They are written from their inception and designed to appear as whole stories.

Note: References throughout are to Robert Fagles' poetic translation, *Homer: The Odyssey* (New York: Penguin Putnam Inc., 1996). Citations are by book and line; for example, line 47 in Book 3 is represented as (3.47).

The Odyssey as Epic

Composed around 700 BC, *The Odyssey* is one of the earliest epics still in existence and, in many ways, sets the pattern for the genre, neatly fitting the definition of a primary epic (that is, one that grows out of oral tradition). The hero is long-suffering Odysseus, king of Ithaca and surrounding islands and hero of the Trojan War. He has been gone 20 years from his homeland, his wife, Penelope, and his son, Telemachus. Odysseus embodies many of the virtues of ancient Greek civilization and in some ways defines them. He is not, however, without his flaws, which sometimes get him into trouble.

Epics usually open with a statement of the subject and an invocation to the Muse or Muses—the nine sister goddesses in Greek mythology, the daughters of the king of gods, Zeus, and Mnemosyne ("Memory"). Certain Muses preside over song and poetry, which are joined in epics. Sometimes Muses are assigned to all the liberal arts and sciences. Clio is usually thought of as the Muse of history. Erato takes care of lyrical love poetry. Calliope is the Muse most often associated with *epic* poetry.

Having invoked the Muse, the epic poet then begins in the middle of the tale; teachers sometimes use a Latin term, *in medias res* ("in the middle of things"), to identify this technique. Beginning in the middle of the action, the poet then fills in significant prior events through flashbacks or narration.

The *Odyssey* also employs most of the literary and poetic devices associated with epics: catalogs, digressions, long speeches, journeys or quests, various trials or tests of the hero, similes, metaphors, and divine intervention.

Although few contemporary authors attempt to compose epics, the influence of the genre and of *The Odyssey* is extensive. Many critics consider James Joyce's *Ulysses* (1922), which uses Odysseus' Latin name ("Ulysses") for the title and places a very flawed non-hero in Dublin, to be the most important novel of the twentieth century. Other works that students might compare to *The Odyssey* include Mark Twain's *Huckleberry Finn* (1884), J. D. Salinger's *The Catcher in the Rye* (1951), John Cheever's short story "The Swimmer" (in the collection *The Brigadier and the Golf Widow*, 1964), and Donald Barthelme's *The Dead Father* (1975).

The Setting of Ithaca

While it includes recollections of earlier times, most of the action in *The Odyssey* takes place in the ten years following the Trojan War. Historically, was there ever such a war? W. A. Camps (*An Introduction to Homer*, 1980, "Preliminary") argues impressively that there probably was but that it was much different from Homer's depiction in *The Iliad* or the recollections of the characters in *The Odyssey*. Archaeological evidence indicates that the war may have taken place around 1220 BC and that the city Homer calls Troy was destroyed by fire. *The Odyssey* was likely composed about five hundred years after these events.

In the interim, countless bards had worked over the stories. What we see (or hear) in Homer, is not a depiction of history but a world created out of legend, folk tales, at least one poet's imagination, and a little bit of history. The "Wanderings of Odysseus," as his travel adventures are often called, take place largely in a reality beyond our own; the settings vary widely. Ithaca, on the other hand, is a constant for Odysseus and Homer's audience.

Politically, the system in Ithaca is less formal than a city-state, but it does provide structure based on power. Odysseus is not just a great warrior or excellent seaman, although those are important talents. He also is the best carpenter that Ithaca has known, the best hunter of wild boar, the finest marksman, and the leading expert on animal husbandry. Odysseus can plow the straightest furrow and mow the largest stretch of meadow in a day. In fact, it is his superior skill, his intelligence, and his prowess that enable him to maintain his power even after many years of absence. As long as he or his reputation can maintain control, Odysseus remains king of Ithaca and surrounding islands.

Along with power, of course, comes wealth. Because Ithaca has no coined money, wealth is measured by livestock, household furnishings, servants, slaves, and treasure. Slavery is not only accepted and encouraged in Homer's world, but slaves are viewed as symbols of wealth and power. Piracy, war, and raids on foreign cities are all accepted means of increasing wealth. The first thing that Odysseus does after leaving Troy, for example, is to sack Ismarus, stronghold of the Cicones. In addition to plunder, he captures the women.

Social traditions are strong in this community; ironically, it is the social tradition of hospitality that proves dangerous for Odyssey's wife, Penelope, and his son, Telemachus.

Finally, the people of Ithaca believe strongly in fate and the right of the gods to alter human life at any time. They hope that virtue will be rewarded, but they accept the vicissitudes of fortune. If an Ithacan stubs his toe in the garden, he may say, "Some god sent that rock to alter my path!" Odysseus himself is proof that, if the gods choose, anything might happen, even to a king.

The Background of the Story

King Odysseus of Ithaca has been gone from home for 20 years. The first 10 he spent fighting heroically and victoriously with the Greeks in the Trojan War; the last 10, he spent trying to get home. From other sources, we know that the goddess Athena arranged for storms to blow the Greeks off course as they attempted to sail home from the war. She was outraged because a Greek warrior had desecrated her temple by attempting to rape Cassandra (daughter of the last king of Troy) in that sacred place. Worse, the Greeks had not punished the man. Although Athena intervenes on Odysseus' behalf repeatedly throughout the epic, her curse originally causes his wanderings.

With Odysseus gone, all that he has—his kingship, his wealth, his home, and his wife and son—is in jeopardy. His wife Penelope finds herself surrounded by unwanted suitors because she is the key to the throne and to Odysseus' wealth. Her new husband would, at the very least, have a distinct advantage in the competition for a new king. Like her son, Telemachus, Penelope lacks the power to eject the suitors who have invaded her home and are bent on forcing her to marry.

In his absence, Odysseus' son, Telemachus, is referred to as the heir apparent and, as such, is constantly in danger, the more so as he becomes a man and is perceived as a threat by his mother's suitors. Telemachus lacks the stature of his father, and although he can summon the Achaeans (Greeks) on the island to full assembly, he cannot accomplish his goals—namely to rid his home of the unwanted suitors who have abused a custom of hospitality. Not only does Telemachus lack power to maintain control, but he also has no formal system of laws or courts to support him. Telemachus himself acknowledges that he may, at best, be ruler only of his own house.

If Telemachus were to assume the crown without sufficient resources to defend it, which he currently lacks, he risk being deposed and, most likely, killed. If Penelope stalls much longer in selecting a suitor, Ithaca could find itself in civil war, and she and her son may well be among its first victims. If she chooses a husband, her son is still in danger unless he is willing to abdicate his claim to the throne. As repugnant as marriage seems, it may be necessary for Ithaca's and (possibly) her son's survival.

A Brief Synopsis

After an invocation to the Muse of poetry, the epic begins *in medias res* ("in the middle of things"). Odysseus has been gone from Ithaca for about 20 years—the first 10 spent fighting the Trojan War, the last 10 trying to get home.

Meanwhile, Odysseus' wife, Penelope, tries to fend off over 100 suitors who have invaded the royal palace, seeking her hand in marriage (and a chance of ruling Ithaca), and indulging in great amounts of food and wine at the hosts' expense. Telemachus, son of Odysseus and Penelope, is just coming of age (he is approximately 21) and is at a loss as to what to do about the suitors. Mother and son yearn for Odysseus' return.

Books 1–4

The first four books deal with Telemachus' struggle (in fact, Odysseus does not appear in the epic until Book 5). A secondary plot in *The Odyssey* is Telemachus' coming of age, his own quest, which scholars sometimes refer to as the "Telemacheia."

The goddess Athena appears to the young prince in disguise and advises him to gather an assembly of the island's leaders to protest the invasion of the suitors. Soon after, he is to visit King Nestor of Pylos and King Menelaus of Sparta, old comrades of his father's, to gather from them any new of Odysseus.

At the assembly, the two leading suitors—the aggressive Antinous and the smooth-talking Eurymachus—confront the prince. They accuse Penelope of delaying too long in her choice of a new husband. Telemachus speaks well but accomplishes little at the assembly because the suitors are from some of the strongest families in the area and are impatient with Penelope's delays.

As Telemachus secretly sets off for Pylos and Sparta, the suitors plot to assassinate him. At Pylos, Telemachus learns little of his father but is encouraged to visit Sparta where King Menelaus reports that Odysseus is alive but held captive by the goddess nymph Calypso.

Books 5–8

Homer leaves the story of Telemachus as the suitors are about to ambush his ship on its return to Ithaca. At Athena's urging, the gods have decided to free Odysseus from Calypso. Hermes, the messenger god, delivers the order to Odysseus' captor. Odysseus has spent seven years with the goddess, sleeping with her at night and pining for his home and family during the day. Calypso is a beautiful, lustful nymph who wants to marry Odysseus and grant him immortality, but he longs for Penelope and Ithaca. Reluctantly, Calypso sends Odysseus on his way.

Poseidon, the sea god, spots the wayfarer and, seeking revenge because Odysseus blinded Poseidon's son Cyclops, shipwrecks Odysseus on Phaeacia, which is ruled by King Alcinous. The Phaeacians, civilized and hospitable people, welcome the stranger and encourage him to tell of his adventures. Through Odysseus' narration, the reader goes back 10 years and hears his tale.

Books 9–12

Known as "The Wanderings of Odysseus," this section is the most famous of the epic. At the end of the Trojan War, Odysseus and his men sail first to the land of the Cicones. The Greeks succeed in raiding the central city but linger too long and are routed by a reserve force. Hoping to sail directly home, the flotilla instead encounters a severe storm, brought on by Athena, that blows them far off course to the land of the Lotus-eaters. These are not hostile people, but eating the lotus plant removes memory and ambition; Odysseus is barely able to pull his men away and resume the journey.

Curiosity compels Odysseus to explore the land of the Cyclops, a race of uncivilized, cannibalistic, one-eyed giants. One of them, Polyphemus (also known simply as "Cyclops"), traps Odysseus' scouting party in his cave. To escape, Odysseus blinds the one-eyed monster, incurring the wrath of the giant's father, Poseidon.

Aeolus, the wind god, is initially a friendly host. He captures all adverse winds and bags them for Odysseus, who is thus able to sail within sight of Ithaca. Unfortunately, his men suspect that the bag holds treasure and open it while Odysseus sleeps. The troublesome winds blow the party back to Aeolus, who wants no more to do with them, speculating that they must be cursed by the gods.

The next hosts, the cannibalistic Laestrygonians, sink all the ships but Odysseus' in a surprise attack. The remaining Greeks reach Aeaea, home of the beautiful enchantress Circe, who turns several of them into pigs. With advice from Hermes, Odysseus cleverly defeats Circe and becomes her lover. She lifts the spell from his men and aids in the group's eventual departure a year later, advising Odysseus that he must sail to the Land of the Dead. There, he receives various Greek heroes, a visit from his own mother, and an important prophecy from the seer Tiresias. Odysseus resumes his journey.

Barely surviving the temptations of the Sirens' songs and an attack by a six-headed monster named Scylla, Odysseus and his crew arrive at the island of the Sungod Helios. Despite severe warnings not to, the men feast on the cattle of the Sungod during Odysseus' brief absence. Zeus is outraged and destroys the ship as the Greeks depart, killing all but Odysseus, who is washed ashore at Calypso's island, where he stays until released seven years later.

Books 13–24

The story of his adventures finished, Odysseus receives the admiration and gifts of the Phaeacians who follow their tradition of returning wayfaring strangers to their homelands by sailing him to Ithaca. Meanwhile, Athena helps Telemachus avoid the suitors' ambush and arranges for him to meet his father at their pig farm not far from the palace.

Reunited with his son and with the assistance of Athena and his faithful swineherd Eumaeus, Odysseus returns to his home palace disguised as a beggar. For the time, he resists striking back at the suitors who insult and assault him. Penelope seems at least suspicious that he is her husband, but it is Eurycleia, a loyal nurse who cared for Odysseus when he was a child, who has no doubt of his identity as she discovers an old scar on his leg when she bathes him.

Penelope arranges a contest, vowing to wed any man who can string the great bow of Odysseus and shoot an arrow through a dozen axes as he used to do. The suitors all fail; only Odysseus himself can perform the feat. With deft planning and more help from Athena, he and Telemachus and two faithful herdsmen slaughter the suitors. Odysseus and Penelope are reunited, as are Odysseus and his aging father, Laertes. Athena makes peace with the suitors' vengeful friends and families, avoiding civil war. Odysseus is home at last.

List of Characters

Human Beings and One Faithful Dog

Odysseus The central figure in the epic, he employs guile as well as courage to return to Ithaca, defeat the suitors, and resume his proper place as king.

Penelope Wife of Odysseus and mother of their son, Telemachus, she is shrewd and faithful in fending off the suitors.

Telemachus Son of Odysseus and Penelope, the prince struggles to gain his own maturity while attempting to deal with the problems of the palace.

Laertes Odysseus' father, the old king lives humbly and in solitude on a small farm where he mourns the absence of his son; once reunited with Odysseus, he is restored to dignity.

Anticleia Odysseus' mother, she dies grieving her son's long absence and sees him only during his visit to the Land of the Dead.

Eurycleia Faithful old nurse to Odysseus (as well as Telemachus), she identifies her master when she recognizes an old scar on his leg.

Eumaeus and Philoetius Odysseus' loyal swineherd and cowherd, they assist him in his return to Ithaca and stand with the king and prince against the suitors.

Argos Trained by Odysseus some twenty years before, the discarded old dog, dying on a dung heap, recognizes his master as Odysseus and Eumaeus approach the palace.

Antinous and Eurymachus The two leading suitors, they differ in that Antinous is more physically aggressive while Eurymachus is a smooth talker.

Eupithes Father of Antinous, he leads the suitors' families and friends who seek revenge for the slaughter and is killed by Laertes.

Melanthius and Melantho Odysseus' *disloyal* goatherd and an insolent palace maidservant, these two are representative of those who serve their master poorly, and each is rewarded with a grisly death.

Agamemnon King of Mycenae and commander of the Greek expedition to Troy, was assassinated by his wife and her lover upon his return home. Homer frequently refers to him, comparing Penelope favorably to Agamemnon's wife, Clytemnestra. Odysseus sees him in the Land of the Dead.

Tiresias The blind seer of Thebes, he meets Odysseus in the Land of the Dead, warns him of impending dangers, offers advice, and foretells a later quest and a long life.

Alcinous King of the Phaeacians, he encourages Odysseus to tell the story of his wanderings and helps the hero return to Ithaca.

Nausicaa Daughter of Alcinous and Queen Arete, she finds Odysseus when he washes ashore on Phaeacia and expresses an attraction toward him.

Gods, Monsters, and Supernatural Beings

Zeus King of the gods, he is somewhat unpredictable but usually supports wayfaring suppliants, hospitality, and his daughter Athena in her concern for Odysseus.

Athena Sometimes called "Pallas Athena" or "Pallas," she frequently intervenes on Odysseus' or Telemachus' behalf, often in disguise and sometimes as Mentor, the prince's adviser.

Polyphemus Also known as "the Cyclops," the one-eyed cannibal giant who traps Odysseus and a scouting party in his cave and is blinded when they escape.

Poseidon God of the sea and father of Polyphemus, he seeks revenge on Odysseus for blinding his son.

Calypso A goddess-nymph, she holds Odysseus captive for seven years, sleeping with him, hoping to marry him, and releasing him only at Zeus' order.

Circe A goddess-enchantress who turns some of Odysseus' crew into swine, she reverses the spell and becomes Odysseus' lover for a year, advising him well when he departs.

Aeolus Master of the winds, he helps Odysseus get within viewing distance of Ithaca but later abandons the voyager, concluding that anyone so unlucky must be cursed.

Character Map

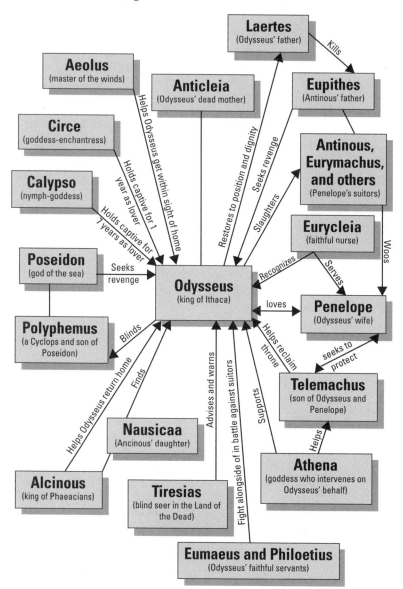

CRITICAL COMMENTARIES

Book 1
Athena Inspires the Prince

Summary

Homer opens *The Odyssey* with an invocation to the Muse of epic poetry and asks for her guidance in telling the story of a man who has experienced many twists and turns of fate and has suffered many hardships. Odysseus, the reader is told, is the only Greek survivor of the Trojan War who has not yet returned home or died trying. He is being held captive on the island Ogygia by the "bewitching nymph" (1.17) Calypso who wants him for her husband. Odysseus has incurred the wrath of Poseidon, god of the sea, by blinding his son Polyphemus the Cyclops. Meanwhile, Odysseus' wife, Penelope, is besieged by suitors at his home in Ithaca.

At a divine council on Mount Olympus, Athena pleads with her father, Zeus, to take pity on Odysseus and allow him to return home. She suggests that Zeus dispatch Hermes to liberate Odysseus from Calypso while Athena visits Ithaca to advise King Odysseus' son, Telemachus.

Disguised as Mentes, an old friend of Odysseus, Athena counsels Telemachus. She predicts that his father will return and insists that the prince must stand up to the suitors and seek more information about Odysseus.

Commentary

Homer uses the epic's opening to introduce the plot, the theme, and the characters of the work. Almost immediately, he delineates two plots that eventually will merge. One is the story of Odysseus who is held captive on Ogygia by Calypso. The other is centered in Ithaca where Odysseus' wife, Penelope, struggles to ward off a number of suitors and hopes for reliable word from or about her husband.

Theme

Homer also introduces several themes that will recur throughout the epic. These include hospitality, reputation, revenge, and power. Throughout, people are responsible for their choices but always susceptible to intervention by the gods.

In the world of Odysseus, one's most treasured possession is his good reputation. One's reputation is determined by how others view him, assessing his character, values, and behavior according to the prevailing social standards and mores. Zeus himself affirms Odysseus' character (1.78–80). Apparently all the gods, except for vengeful Poseidon, hold Odysseus in high regard. Athena, whose curse initially caused Odysseus' wanderings, now wants to forgive and bring him home. When Athena (in disguise) visits Ithaca, she first receives a hospitable welcome from Telemachus (1.144–46) and then gets the usual barrage of questions that strangers face throughout the epic (1.197–204), which are designed to elicit indications of reputation.

The social concept of hospitality is essential to both major plots in *The Odyssey*. (In fact, this concept was also the reason for the Trojan War in *The Iliad*. Paris breaches the hospitality of King Menalaus when he runs off with—or steals—Menelaus' wife, Helen, and takes her back to Troy with him.) In *The Odyssey*, the reader first sees hospitality exploited by Penelope's suitors. They have turned Odysseus' home into their own private party hall and spend most of their time feasting and drinking at the host's expense.

Underlying the theme of revenge is the situation at Odysseus' household. The suitors would not dare such offensive behavior if Odysseus were around or if they anticipated his return. They think he is dead. Only a few (Antinous and Eurymachus chief among them) have any real hope of marrying Penelope and, through that union, have a better chance of becoming the new king. The rest are simply taking advantage of the situation. If Telemachus is initially hesitant about taking action, Athena is not. She incites action in the youthful prince and wishes a "blood wedding" (1.308) on the would-be grooms. It is time for Telemachus to stand up.

Antinous broaches the topic of power when he challenges Telemachus' capacity to reign (1.441–44). He sardonically acknowledges the prince's right to rule but hopes that Zeus will never make Telemachus king of Ithaca. In fact, as Fagles and Knox point out (p. 504), Telemachus probably would not inherit the crown; he would have to earn it. If the showdown were immediate, it seems unlikely that

Telemachus could defeat Antinous either personally or with his few supporters. He would accept the crown if it were the will of Zeus, but his modesty is justified at this point when he says he would simply hope to rule his own household. However, Telemachus senses that Mentes is really Athena and is emboldened by her support. He calls for a full assembly the next morning.

Glossary

(Here and in the following chapters, difficult words and phrases, as well as allusions and historical references, are explained.)

Troy an ancient city in Troas, northwestern Asia Minor, site of the Trojan War.

Ethiopians the people of Ethiopia, an empire in eastern Africa.

Poseidon in Greek mythology, god of the sea, younger brother of Zeus.

Hermes herald and messenger of the gods, guide of deceased souls to the Land of the Dead.

Ogygia Calypso's island in the middle of the sea.

Book 2
Telemachus Sets Sail

Summary

When the assembly gathers the next day, wise old Aegyptius points out that the group has not met in session since King Odysseus left for the Trojan War some 20 years before. He commends the citizen who was bold enough to call for the meeting. Encouraged, Telemachus effectively makes his case against the suitors and asks them to desist. Silence falls across the gathering as most of the men seem moved by the prince's plea.

Insolently, Antinous, the leading suitor, denies responsibility and puts the blame on that "queen of cunning," Penelope (2.95). He tells the legendary tale of the shroud that Penelope wove for the eventual funeral of Odysseus' father, Laertes, the former king now living on a farm where he grieves his son's absence.

Considering the attack on his mother, Telemachus remains surprisingly calm in his rebuttal. But he foreshadows later events by appealing to Zeus for assistance in vengeance. Dueling eagles suddenly swoop near the assembly, which the seer Halitherses interprets as a sign of Odysseus' return. Eurymachus, the other leading suitor, rudely interrupts the aging prophet and threatens Telemachus. Mentor speaks for Telemachus, but the assembly reaches no clear decision and dissolves. With the aid of Athena, who poses as Mentor and sometimes as Telemachus himself, the prince secretly prepares and sets sail for Pylos.

Commentary

Style & Language

Homer effectively uses the content and style of the speeches at the assembly to reveal the types and natures of the characters in the action. Bolstered by Athena, Telemachus takes the speaker's staff and demonstrates that he is quickly becoming a man capable of speaking up to the suitors. The speech moves most of the assembly to silence as the prince presents his case. His initial appeal is emotional as well as informative. Men frequently are moved to tears in the epic, and

Telemachus ends his oration by dashing the speaker's scepter and weeping with passion.

Antinous, however, shockingly insults the queen, whom he obviously wants to marry for mainly political reasons. Penelope, he says, has misguided the suitors for nearly four years now, leading on each man with hints and promises but choosing no one. Antinous demands that Telemachus must send his mother back to her father's home so that the old man might choose a husband for her.

Character Insight

The story of the loom symbolizes the queen's cunning as well as the suitors' density. For three full years, Penelope worked at weaving a shroud for her father-in-law's eventual funeral. She claimed that she would make a decision as soon as the shroud was finished. By day, the renowned weaver worked on a great loom in the royal halls. At night, she secretly unraveled what she had done, amazingly deceiving the young suitors who apparently were too slow of wit or too drunk to discover the ruse. The plot failed only when one of Penelope's servants betrayed her and told the suitors what was happening.

Literary Device

Despite the insults, Telemachus remains calm and counters the leading suitor with logic. He argues that Penelope's father and the public at large would condemn him if he kicked his own mother out of her home. The gods would never tolerate such behavior. Besides, Icarius, the queen's father, lives much too far away. Speaking like an experienced veteran, the prince builds to a passionate peroration, again demanding that the suitors leave. He sarcastically suggests that they might stay if the food and drink are so much better at the royal house of Odysseus; but if they do, he will call on Zeus for vengeance. As if on cue, the king of gods sends eagles as an omen.

Eurymachus, the other leading suitor, is not convinced. Although he later will prove to be a sly manipulator when cornered, here, Eurymachus has no fear and insolently dismisses omens, Odysseus, and the prince. He and the suitors will do whatever they want. It is for others to adjust to them.

In the end, the meeting serves to reveal the suitors to the public, but nothing is done about them. The assembly is an early, somewhat weak example of representative government. It anticipates the later democracies of Athens and other Greek city-states. Despite ruling by power, kings are not absolute monarchs. Their peers influence and sometimes approve or disapprove of policy. Nor is the crown necessarily heredi-tary. It is won by strength, wealth, and conquest. Thus Antinous and Eurymachus think they might rule, especially if either can wed Pene-lope. She, on the other hand, stalls for three reasons: a hope for Odysseus' return, a desire to avoid civil war, and a real concern for her son's safety. Her marriage would force a showdown for the crown, and Telemachus' position is considerably weaker, at this point, than that of the top suitors.

Athena continues to support Telemachus. She inspired the assem-bly meeting, and she plans his secret departure for Pylos, recognizing that the suitors are becoming dangerous and might attempt to assassi-nate him. She disguises herself as Telemachus to gather 20 fine young men and procure a ship. At other times, she appears as Mentor, a trusted counsel whose name inspired our current use of the word. Under the guise of Mentor, she accompanies the prince to Pylos.

Glossary

Achaeans here, a collective name for all Greeks, including Ithacans.

suitors here, the men attempting to court Penelope.

Argive another term for Greek.

Pylos a seaport in the southwestern Peloponnesus in southern Greece, capital city of King Nestor.

Sparta inland city in southern Peloponnesus, located in Laconia, home of King Menelaus and Queen Helen.

pernicious deadly, destructive.

Book 3
King Nestor Remembers

Summary

As Telemachus and Athena (still disguised as Mentor) arrive at Pylos, they come upon a huge ceremony in which some 4,500 people offer 81 bulls in sacrifice to Poseidon. Telemachus feels awkward and embarrassed by his youth and inexperience, but under Athena/Mentor's guidance, he makes a favorable impression on King Nestor, oldest of the Greek chieftains. Nestor's situation and, indeed, the whole state of affairs in Pylos stand in stark contrast to Odysseus' and Ithaca. Through these experiences in Pylos and with Athena's guidance, Telemachus learns how to comport himself as the son and heir to a great king.

Nestor talks of the old days and significantly elaborates on the story of Agamemnon's murder. He has little to offer regarding Odysseus, having last seen Ithaca's king shortly after the victory at Troy, but he suggests that Telemachus and Nestor's son Pisistratus proceed to Sparta to visit Menelaus, Agamemnon's brother, who may be of more help to the guests. Athena returns to the ship to instruct the crew before she leaves on other errands. After another sacrificial feast, Nestor provides a chariot and team of steeds for the two princes' journey to Sparta.

Commentary

The first four books of *The Odyssey* are known to scholars as the "Telemacheia"; they deal with the young prince's quest for information about his father as well as his own journey toward manhood. In the latter sense, this section of the epic is very much a coming-of-age story. Athena/Mentor is a helpful guide to the prince's decorum and always aware that Telemachus must quickly become a man and a warrior.

In addition to hospitality, two themes dominate the visit with Nestor: loyalty to human comrades and family, and devotion to the gods. Throughout *The Odyssey*, Homer's characters refer to Agamemnon's story several times. The tale of Agamemnon's death stands in contrast to events in Ithaca but also serves as a warning of what can happen when loyalty goes awry. Telemachus, growing in the social graces and truly wanting to learn, encourages Nestor's account of the murder of Agamemnon.

Agamemnon was a great warrior, commander of the Greek forces, and chief of their largest contingent at Troy. When he went to war, he left his cousin Aegisthus in charge at home in Mycenae. Motivated by greed and lust, Aegisthus betrayed this trust and seduced Agamemnon's wife, Clytemnestra. The two illicit lovers murdered the great warrior upon his return from the Trojan War. Menelaus, Agamemnon's brother, was absent and thus unable to avenge his death. Later, Agamemnon's children, Orestes (his son) and Electra (his daughter), gained vengeance by killing Aegisthus and the queen. Homer's audience would recognize the widely known story, which later appeared in the works of Sophocles, Aeschylus, Euripides, and the twentieth-century American dramatist Eugene O'Neill, among others. While Penelope's character contrasts with Clytemnestra's in virtue and loyalty, suitors such as Antinous and Eurymachus echo the sinister Aegisthus.

Just as Nestor's tale of Agamemnon's fate underscores the importance of human loyalty, the visit itself illustrates the importance of devotion to the gods. Nestor expresses this devotion through sacrificial feasts. The first thing that Telemachus notices upon arrival at Pylos is the huge celebration in honor of Poseidon. Before the prince leaves with Pisistratus for Sparta, Nestor holds another sacrificial feast in honor of Athena, whom, he realizes, has honored him with a visit. To the Greeks, such displays of devotion were important because the Greeks thought of the gods as being functioning parts of their daily lives in matters both great and small. Pleasing the gods was a practical, as well as a spiritual, endeavor.

Glossary

King Priam king of Troy, killed when the city fell to the Greeks.

flotilla a small fleet of ships or small boats.

Myrmidons legendary Greek warriors of ancient Thessaly who followed their king, Achilles, into the Trojan War.

Mycenae Agamemnon's capital city, in the northeastern Peloponnesus of ancient Greece.

libations liquids poured in offering to a god or gods as part of a religious ritual.

Cauconians people living to the southwest of Pylos.

Book 4
The King and Queen of Sparta

Summary

When they arrive at Sparta, Telemachus and Pisistratus are warmly welcomed. Telemachus is moved to tears by Menelaus' recollections of his friend Odysseus. The king and queen recall some of Odysseus' exploits at Troy but postpone serious talk until the next day. In the morning, Menelaus expresses outrage at the behavior of Penelope's suitors and encourages Telemachus by telling him that Odysseus is alive and a captive of Calypso.

Back in Ithaca, the suitors have discovered that Telemachus is gone and plan to ambush his ship on its return. Penelope is distraught to learn of her son's trip and the planned assassination but is soothed by a vision sent by Athena. Homer leaves the plot of Telemachus dangling as selected suitors board a vessel to set up the surprise attack.

Commentary

Literary
Device

Menelaus' queen is the same Helen whose abduction from Sparta caused the Trojan War. Foreshadowing Odysseus' disguise when he returns to Ithaca, Helen recalls how he scarred his body and donned slave's clothing in order to slip into Troy under the guise of a beggar. Still with the Trojans at that time, she alone suspected that the beggar was a spy; but she protected his secret until he was safely gone. Menelaus recalls the crafty Odysseus' legendary ruse of the Trojan horse that led to the defeat of Troy.

Although thrilled to hear these stories, Telemachus is more encouraged by Menelaus' revelation, the next day, that Odysseus may yet live. In order to learn his own way home to Sparta, Menelaus, marooned in Egypt, had to trap Proteus, Poseidon's servant and a shape-shifter who can instantly turn himself into a serpent, panther, boar, tree, or even a torrent of water. Proteus' daughter, a sea-nymph, told Menelaus how to catch her father and get the truth from him. In addition to learning his own way home, Menelaus also learned that Odysseus was alive and a captive of Calypso on Ogygia.

Over the centuries, some scholars have asserted that no one poet could have presented the world of *The Iliad* and that of *The Odyssey*. In *The Iliad,* many of the same characters as those found in *The Odyssey* are filled with the vigor of youth and devoted to the honors of war or the thrills of lust. Helen is an example. She was, as Christopher Marlowe would write more than 2,000 years after the creation of *The Odyssey*, " . . . the face that launched a thousand ships, / And burnt the topless towers of Ilium" (*The Tragical History of Doctor Faustus*, 1604)— the woman whose abduction was the catalyst for the Trojan War. Although she is still quite striking (4.136) in *The Odyssey*, she is a matronly, middle-aged hostess, far different from the Helen who drove men to such desire that they were willing to go to war for her. However, the disparity between her portrayal in *The Iliad* and that in *The Odyssey* need not be interpreted as evidence against a single author. Instead, it merely marks the passage of time—approximately 20 years. Helen, like all the principals from the Trojan War who are still alive, is simply older. The amazing thing about Odysseus is that, despite the passage of years, he will be able rise to the insult of the suitors and once more take arms as he did in his prime.

Glossary

Zeus king of the gods in ancient Greek mythology.

Olympus highest mountain in Greece and legendary home of the gods.

Aphrodite goddess of love and beauty, daughter of Zeus.

Pharos island near the mouth of Egypt's Nile river.

Proteus the "Old Man of the Sea," a sea god and servant of Poseidon known for his ability to change shape.

Ajax [4.560] the Greek warrior whose offense at Athena's temple resulted in Odysseus' wanderings; not to be confused with the Great Ajax, whom Odysseus defeated in the contest for Achilles' armor.

Book 5
Odysseus—Nymph and Shipwreck

Summary

The gods have gathered again on Olympus. Poseidon is notably absent, and Athena once more advocates Odysseus' case. Zeus agrees to send his son Hermes immediately to Ogygia in order to liberate the king of Ithaca from Calypso. Zeus advises Athena to help Telemachus return home unharmed, escaping the suitors' ambush.

On Ogygia, Calypso, aware that she must not cross Zeus, begrudgingly agrees to follow Hermes' directions. She provides a raft and supplies for Odysseus but no escort.

The hero himself is first seen weeping on a beach " . . . as always, / wrenching his heart with sobs and groans and anguish, / gazing out over the barren sea through blinding tears" (5.93–95). Odysseus wants to go home. At first understandably skeptical of Calypso's offer of freedom, he soon joins preparations for his departure.

Poseidon, returning from a visit to Ethiopia, spots Odysseus on the open sea, raises his trident, and sends a swamping storm that nearly drowns him. With the help of Athena and a sea nymph named Leucothea, Odysseus makes it ashore on the island of Scheria, home of the Phaeacians.

Commentary

Throughout the epic, Homer casually reveals upcoming events in a way that confirms the theory that the audience is already familiar with the plot. He does so again early in Book 5 (5.33 ff) when he speaks of Odysseus' future while giving orders to Hermes.

The poet's talent is shown in the *manner* in which he spins the yarn. One of his favorite devices is rhetoric, effective manipulation of language, especially in the characters' public speeches. One example is in the gathering of the assembly on Ithaca in Book 2. Another example is Athena's plea to Zeus in the divine assembly on Olympus at the beginning of Book 5. Considering that *The Odyssey* is one of the earliest examples of Western literature still in existence, the level of rhetoric is quite sophisticated.

Athena convincingly employs irony to make her point. She suggests that Zeus and the other gods never again allow a mortal king to be kind or just since Odysseus' fate has established that those characteristics are not rewarded. He has lost his ships and crew, is abandoned on Ogygia, and his son's life is in jeopardy. Athena is just warming to the theme when Zeus interrupts her. Like a convinced judge as well as an indulgent father, he concedes her case and suggests that they move on with her plan to free Odysseus.

Because Book 5 presents the reader's first meeting with Odysseus, it is interesting that Homer chooses to show him alone on a beach on Calypso's island, apparently defeated and weeping. Throughout the poem, Odysseus is a series of apparent contradictions, a much more complicated character than we would find in any stereotypical epic hero.

The modern reader might be bothered by the apparent double standard of morality in the epic, in which Penelope is expected to be absolutely celibate for 20 years, rejecting all suitors and faithfully awaiting her husband's return, while Odysseus has at least two extended sexual liaisons. When the reader first meets him on Ogygia, he has been spending the nights in Calypso's bed and his days mourning his absence from home and family. Homer's audiences would not have had difficulty reconciling these differences. Odysseus *does* want to return to Penelope and his life on Ithaca despite the obvious attractions—physical, spiritual, and mortal—that Calypso has to offer him. It does not occur to Odysseus or his contemporary audience that he has one code of behavior for himself and another for Penelope.

Calypso rages at the double standard when Hermes announces that she must let Odysseus go. She launches into a rant against the male gods, "unrivaled lords of jealousy" (5.131), who think nothing of gods carousing with mortal women but condemn female gods when they take mortal lovers. She cites an impressive litany of examples. However, in the end, she must accede to the judgment of Zeus.

Glossary

Tithonus in ancient Greek mythology, husband of Dawn.

Pieria region located north of Mount Olympus.

pungent having a sharp or piercing taste or smell; also, causing sharp pain, especially to the feelings.

ambrosia food of the gods, thought to grant immortality.

Orion mythological hunter or the constellation named after him.

Styx one of the rivers of the Land of the Dead across which the souls of the dead are ferried.

Pleiades, Plowman, Great Bear, and Hunter constellations.

Books 6–8

The Princess and the Stranger; Phaeacia's Halls and Gardens; A Day for Songs and Contests

Summary

King Alcinous and Queen Arete rule the seafaring Phaeacians on the island of Scheria. The morning after Odysseus' rugged landing, Athena (disguised as a friend) sends their daughter, Nausicaa, and some of her handmaidens to wash clothes near the spot where the beleaguered hero has collapsed.

Nausicaa is a classic nubile beauty and seems attracted to the wayfaring stranger. She tells him how to find the palace and endear himself to the queen, thus insuring his safe passage home. Odysseus follows her instructions and is received hospitably at the royal household. It is important to note that Odysseus refrains from assuming the position of a suppliant with Nausicaa, perhaps because she lacks any real power to help him, perhaps because dropping to his knees and hugging her legs might be embarrassingly intimate for the young maiden and cause her to take offense. He has no such reservations with Queen Arete and is granted mercy.

Odysseus eventually reveals his identity and welcomes the Phaeacians' offer to return him to Ithaca. First, however, he tells them of his wanderings. These stories take up the next four books (Books 9–12), the best known part of the epic.

Commentary

The Phaeacian section of *The Odyssey* seems most likely influenced by fairy tales or folk legends. It fits a genre, found in many cultures, in which a beautiful, innocent young girl, often a princess, is attracted to a rugged, handsome stranger who usually is older and always more experienced. Sometimes the two end up together; more often, the man makes an impression on the younger woman (with varying degrees of intimacy) and moves on. Even in modern times, this theme is popular in fiction and drama. In this case, Odysseus acknowledges the charms of the virgin Nausicaa but is intent on returning to Penelope.

Phaeacia certainly is a Utopia. With minor exceptions, the people are decent, civilized, and kind. They are known for returning helpless strangers to their homelands, an act that exceeds even the generous welcomes usually found in *The Odyssey*. This tradition is also consistent with the locals' devotion to Zeus, protector of lost wanderers and champion of suppliants. The island itself is a paradise. Luxuriant orchards, featuring apples, pears, figs, pomegranates, and more, bear fruit year-round (7.129 ff.). Vegetables and grains are in abundance. No one goes hungry on Scheria.

The Phaeacians are not great warriors, but they excel at seamanship, dancing, and sports. During an exhibition of athletic skills, a youngster called Broadsea embarrasses King Alcinous by openly mocking Odysseus and challenging his athletic skills. The great Ithacan promptly hurls a discus farther than any of the younger men can manage. He is equally adept at wit and conversation, convincing his hosts that he is no ordinary wayfarer. When Demodocus, the blind bard, sings of the exploits of those at Troy, Odysseus weeps, causing King Alcinous to suspect that a hero of the Trojan War is among them. Odysseus finally identifies himself and agrees to recount the story of his wanderings.

A recurring theme throughout the epic is the conflict between appearance and reality. Athena is a master of disguise, appropriately appearing in whatever form best suits her purpose. She is also one of the first great makeover artists. When a character under her care, such as Telemachus or Odysseus, needs to look impressive, she devotes her talents to the task. As he prepares for the celebration in his honor (8.20–22), for example, Athena makes him look taller, more massive, more splendid in every way. Of course, the hero of the Trojan War is no stranger to disguise. He posed as a beggar to enter Troy and initiated the ruse of the giant wooden horse filled with Greek warriors, a story retold here (8.559 ff.) by Demodocus. Odysseus' return to Ithaca will be eased by further disguise. Throughout the story of his wanderings, which he is about to recite, the theme of appearance versus reality complicates and enriches his quest.

Glossary

Artemis goddess of the hunt, twin sister of Apollo.

brine sea water, salt water.

Apollo god of archery.

sceptered invested with authority or sovereignty.

Ares god of war, lover of Aphrodite.

Book 9
In the One-Eyed Giant's Cave

Summary

After identifying himself to the Phaeacians at the feast, Odysseus tells the story of his wanderings. Following the victory at Troy, he and his men sail to Ismarus, the stronghold of the Cicones. With apparent ease, they sack the city, kill the men, enslave the women, and enjoy a rich haul of plunder. Odysseus advises his men to leave immediately with their riches, but they ignore his warnings. The Cicones gather reinforcements, counterattack, and eventually rout the Greeks. Odysseus and his men retreat by sea. Storms blow the ships off course, but they finally arrive at the land of the Lotus-eaters. The inhabitants are not hostile; however, eating the lotus plant causes Odysseus' men to lose memory and all desire to return home. Odysseus barely gets them back to sea. The next stop is the land of the Cyclops, lawless one-eyed giants. One of them, Polyphemus, traps Odysseus and a scouting party in his cave. Only the Greek hero's wily plan allows escape.

Commentary

Literary Device

Readers should not confuse Odysseus' pride in identifying himself to the Phaeacian hosts with vanity. One's name and reputation are crucial in the Homeric world. When Odysseus states that his "fame has reached the skies" (9.22), he is merely stating fact, identifying himself. Reputation is of paramount importance in this culture. But his pride in his name foreshadows Odysseus' questionable judgment in identifying himself during the escape from Polyphemus.

The next four books (Books 9–12) deal with the hero's wanderings and are the most widely known in the epic. Odysseus does not discuss, at this point, *why* he was blown off course and unable to return directly to Ithaca. Phemius, the renowned Ithacan bard, outlines the tale early in *The Odyssey* (1.375–76) when he performs "The Achaeans' Journey Home from Troy." The details are not articulated there either, but the story of Ajax's attempted rape of Cassandra in Athena's temple and the lack of punishment meted out to him by the Greeks would have been well known by Homer's audience.

Theme

Many critics see Odysseus' wanderings as a series of trials or tests through which the hero attains a certain wisdom and prepares to be a great king as well as a great warrior. If so, then *judgment* seems to be a key. If Odysseus is to survive, he must ultimately become wise as well as courageous and shrewd.

The first test is against the Cicones. Some scholars suggest that Odysseus raids Ismarus because the Cicones are allies of the Trojans. Others conclude that he sacks the city simply because it is there. Certainly piracy and marauding were legitimate professions for Ithacans. At question is not the raid but Odysseus' men's foolish disregard for his advice. Having gained victory and considerable plunder, Odysseus wants to be on his way. His men, on the other hand, drink and feast as the Cicones gather reinforcements, skilled warriors who eventually rout the Greeks. Odysseus loses six men from each of his ships and is lucky to get away by sea.

Odysseus escapes, but storms and a strong north wind drive his ships off course. As he rounds Cape Malea (near Cythera, north and slightly west of Crete), he needs only to swing north by northwest 300 miles or so to be home. The winds drive him away. Nine days later, he reaches the land of the Lotus-eaters. (Homeric geography is suspect, but some scholars place this at or near Libya.)

Students familiar with some of the legends of *The Odyssey* but new to the epic itself might be surprised to see that the section on the Lotus-eaters is only about twenty-five lines long (9.92–107). Homer has touched on a universal theme, the lure of oblivion through drugs. The Lotus-eaters have no interest in killing the Greeks; the danger is the lotus and the forgetfulness it causes. This time, Odysseus' judgment prevails, and he manages to get his men back to sea before too many are seduced by the honey-sweet fruit that wipes out ambition and memory.

Character Insight

The Cyclops, whom the wanderers visit next, contrast most vividly with the Phaeacians. The Phaeacians once lived near the Cyclops but moved to Scheria to avoid the lawless brutes. While the Phaeacians are civilized and peace loving, the Cyclops have no laws, no councils, and no interest in civility or hospitality. It is during this episode that Odysseus' judgment comes into question. Having feasted on goat meat on an offshore island, Odysseus and his men could move on. However, Odysseus is curious about who lives on the mainland. Taking a dozen of his best men, as well as a skin of extremely strong wine that he received from a priest of Apollo, Odysseus sets out to investigate a cavern near the mainland shore. It is the lair of Polyphemus, a Cyclops. Discovering abundant food in the cave, the men want to raid it and sail off, but Odysseus insists on staying to try the hospitality of the owner, who proves to be no charming host.

Polyphemus, a son of Poseidon and nearly as powerful as the gods himself, scoffs at the concept of hospitality and welcomes his guests by devouring two for supper and trapping the rest inside his cave for later meals. When the Cyclops leaves, Odysseus devises a plan. From an olive-wood that the giant uses as a club, the Greeks fashion a pointed lance about a fathom (six feet) long and char the point to hardness. When Cyclops returns that night, he downs two more men for supper, and Odysseus offers him the skin's contents. The arrogant giant swills down three large bowls full.

As he is drinking, the Cyclops demands to know Odysseus' name. The wily hero says that it is "Nobody" (*outis* in the Greek). When the giant passes out, the Greeks immediately seize their opportunity and grind the lance into the Cyclops' single eye, blinding him. The monster screams with pain and cries for help, but when other Cyclops arrive outside and ask who is harming him, Polyphemus can only answer, "*Nobody,* . . . Nobody's killing me now by fraud and not by force!" (9.454–55). The next morning, when Polyphemus, blind, lets his rams out in the morning, Odysseus and his men ride out with them, tucked under their bellies and using the animals as shields.

Character Insight

As Odysseus and his men sail away, however, Odysseus again employs questionable judgment, shouting taunts at the wounded monster. Using the Greek's voice to direct his aim, Polyphemus hurls giant boulders after the ship, barely missing. Then Odysseus assures that his trials will continue by boasting to Polyphemus that it was he, Odysseus of Ithaca, not a "Nobody," who gouged out the giant's eye. In this instance, Odysseus is not simply showing pride in his good name, but foolish arrogance that allows the monster to identify him. Polyphemus then calls on his father, Poseidon, god of the sea, to avenge him. In a curse repeated by Tiresias as a prophecy (11.125–35) and by Circe as a warning (12.148–53), Polyphemus asks Poseidon to see that Odysseus never makes it home. Or, if the Fates have already determined that he must, then may he arrive late, broken, and alone, finding great troubles in his household (9.590–95). With nothing but oceans between him and Ithaca and the god of the sea as his new enemy, Odysseus has paid a hefty price for his pride.

Glossary

Ismarus an ancient seaport on the Aegean Sea, north and slightly west of Troy, home of the Cicones.

Malea southeastern cape of the Peloponnesus.

Cythera a Greek island located between the Peloponnesus and Crete.

fathom a unit of length equal to six feet, used to measure the depth of water.

dam the female parent of any four-legged animal.

bellwether a ram, usually castrated, that wears a bell around its neck and is followed by the other sheep.

Book 10
The Bewitching Queen of Aeaea

Summary

Having escaped the Cyclops, Odysseus and his men arrive at the home of Aeolus, master of the winds, where they are greeted warmly and hosted for a month. Eager to move on, Odysseus receives an ox-skin pouch from Aeolus. In it are captured all the winds that might drive the ships off course. Only the West Wind is left free to blow them toward Ithaca. After ten days of sailing, the Greeks are so close to home that they can actually see men tending fires on their island. Exhausted, Odysseus falls asleep. Curious and suspicious, his men open the ox skin expecting to find treasure and inadvertently release heavy squalls that blow them right back to Aeolus' island. The wind god refuses to help them further.

With no favoring wind at all, the Greeks must row, and they come upon the land of the Laestrygonians, cannibalistic giants who suddenly attack and devour the seamen, hurling boulders at the ships and spearing the men like so many fish. Only Odysseus' vessel escapes. It sails to the island of Aeaea, home of the beautiful but dangerous goddess Circe, whom Odysseus can overcome only through the intervention of Hermes, messenger of the gods and son of Zeus.

Commentary

Judgment is once more a crucial problem as the Greeks very nearly get home to Ithaca only to see their goal vanish in a storm. Aeolus is impressed with Odysseus and treats him with classic hospitality. He harnesses all potentially destructive winds, binding them tightly in an ox skin and stowing the ox skin onboard Odysseus' ship. However, as he did following the initial victory over the Cicones, Odysseus loses control of his men. While he sleeps, curiosity and mistrust overcome them. They suspect that the ox skin contains great treasure, which they feel should be shared. Tragically, they release all the adverse winds and are blown back to Aeolus. The god of the winds refuses to help Odysseus further because he infers that the gods must despise anyone so unlucky.

Odysseus understandably despairs as storms blow him away from Ithaca, but he manages to resist the temptation to commit suicide (10.55–61).

Things only get worse as the flotilla, with no favoring wind from Aeolus, rows to the land of the Laestrygonians. Odysseus cautiously sends scouts to check out the inhabitants who initially seem hospitable. Suddenly the hosts devour the scouts and attack Odysseus' ships. They hurl huge boulders, reminiscent of the attack by Cyclops, and spear the seamen like fish. Only Odysseus' cool leadership permits his single ship to row to safety.

Caution and judgment, some of it from the gods, eventually save most of the remaining crew at Circe's island of Aeaea. Odysseus again sends out a scouting party. To their delight, they are greeted by what appears to be a beautiful, hospitable goddess with magical charm and a spellbinding voice. Circe calls them into her halls and gives them a potion that, like the lotus, erases from their memories any thoughts of home. Then she strikes them with her wand and turns them into swine, driving them into her pigsties. Only Eurylochus is suspicious enough to stand back and escape. His report to Odysseus stirs the always admirable courage of the leader, who immediately sets out alone to attempt rescue.

Courage alone, however, won't save the day. Hermes, disguised as a young man, intervenes and tells Odysseus how to overcome Circe: He must take a magic herb, moly, which will serve as antidote to Circe's potions. When the goddess wields her wand, Odysseus is to pull his sword and attack, not cower, as if he will run her through. Circe will then surrender and offer her considerable sexual favors to Odysseus. He must accept but only after securing promises from the goddess that she will release his men and hereafter treat them all well.

The events unfold as Hermes predicts, and life is good for Odysseus and his men for the next year as they feast and drink. Odysseus, as Hermes predicts, shares the bed of a goddess.

The crew eventually wants to move on and convinces Odysseus to resume the journey home. Circe keeps her promise to help them but advises that they first must visit the Land of the Dead (*Hades* in some translations) to consult with the spirit of the blind prophet Tiresias. The goddess offers instructions and supplies for the journey. With some misgivings, the Greeks set sail for the ends of the earth.

Glossary

squalls brief, sudden, and violent windstorms.

Perse a sea nymph, wife of the Sungod (Helios) and mother of Circe.

Pramnian a type of wine often used in potions or medicines.

moly an herb of magic powers.

nymph a female nature spirit or goddess.

Persephone queen of the underworld.

sodden thoroughly saturated, drunk.

Book 11
The Kingdom of the Dead

Summary

The Land of the Dead is near the homes of the Cimmerians, who live "shrouded in mist and cloud" (11.17), never seeing the sun. Odysseus follows Circe's instructions, digging a trench at the site prescribed and pouring libations of milk, honey, mellow wine, and pure water. He ceremoniously sprinkles barley and then sacrifices a ram and a ewe, the dark blood flowing into the trench to attract the dead.

First to approach is Elpenor, one of Odysseus' men who died just before the crew left Circe's home. Elpenor had spent the last night in a drunken stupor on Circe's roofs, breaking his neck as he fell off when he arose at dawn. Because of the urgency of Odysseus' journey to the Land of the Dead, Elpenor was left unburied, and his spirit requests proper rites when the Greeks return to Aeaea. Others are drawn to the blood: Odysseus' mother, Anticleia; Tiresias the prophet; and old comrades Agamemnon and Achilles, among others.

Commentary

Literary Device

The journey to the Land of the Dead—where the dead ("souls") receive reciprocity ("Justice")—is not so much a test for Odysseus as it is an epiphany. His mortality is put in context as he watches the shades of warrior comrades, legendary figures, and even his own mother. Following instructions, he must speak with Tiresias, the blind seer from Thebes, before he can allow his mother or any others to approach. Drinking the blood temporarily revitalizes the dead; briefly they can communicate with Odysseus and speak only truth.

Tiresias observes that one of the gods, the earth shaker (Poseidon), is angry with Odysseus for blinding his son (Polyphemus, the Cyclops) and will cause Odysseus and his men many problems. However, Tiresias reports, the Greeks can get home alive if they use proper judgment and control. Above all, they must not harm the cattle of Helios, the Sungod, no matter the temptation. If they do, Odysseus' men will die. Echoing the curse of the Cyclops (9.590–95), Tiresias warns that Odysseus himself might eventually arrive home, but he will be "a broken man—all shipmates lost" (11.130) and find his household in disarray. Furthermore, the prophet instructs Odysseus that he must eventually pursue yet another quest, carrying his oar inland until he meets a race of men who know so little about the sea that they think the oar is "a fan to winnow grain" (11.146). At that place, Odysseus is to make certain sacrifices to Poseidon. If he follows these and other instructions, Odysseus can live out his life and die in peace. (The journey inland, however, takes place after the events told of in *The Odyssey*.)

Odysseus' own mother, who died of grief and longing for him, is allowed to approach only after his audience with the seer. Until seeing her among the dead, Odysseus was unaware of his mother's death. She tells him of his father, Laertes, who still lives but similarly grieves and has lost his will. In one of the most moving scenes in the epic, Odysseus tries three times to hold his mother but cannot because she is no longer flesh and blood.

Literary
Device

Agamemnon and Achilles, comrades of Odysseus at Troy, are among the many other dead who approach. Agamemnon tells the story of his murder by his wife, Clytemnestra, and her paramour, Aegisthus, a story referred to repeatedly throughout the epic, effectively contrasting the murderous infidelity of Clytemnestra with the dedicated loyalty of Penelope.

More controversial is Achilles' appearance because it contradicts the heroic ideal of death with honor, resulting in some form of glorious immortality. Here, Achilles' attitude is that death is death; he would rather be a living slave to a tenant farmer than king of the dead. His only solace is to hear that his son fares well in life.

The dead flock toward Odysseus. He is overwhelmed and welcomes his departure, feeling that, whatever his struggles in life might be, he prefers them to residence in the Land of the Dead.

Glossary

Creon king of Thebes, successor to Oedipus.

Oedipus Abandoned at birth and raised by the king of Corinth, he unwittingly killed his father and married his mother.

Leda a queen of Sparta and the mother, by Zeus in the form of a swan, of Helen and Pollux.

Crete an island in the Mediterranean off the southeastern coast of Greece.

Achilles famed warrior, hero of Homer's *Iliad*.

Tantalus a king punished in Hades by having to stand in water that recedes when he bends to drink it and beneath fruit that ascends when he reaches to eat it.

Sisyphus a cruel king condemned in Hades to the eternal, frustrating effort of rolling a huge stone uphill, only to have it always roll down again.

Book 12
The Cattle of the Sun

Summary

True to his word, Odysseus returns to Aeaea for Elpenor's funeral rites. Circe is helpful once more, providing supplies and warnings about the journey to begin the next dawn. First the Greeks must get past the Sirens whose irresistible songs lure sailors into their island's coastal reefs. Next they must avoid the Clashing Rocks (called "Wandering Rocks" or "Rovers" in some translations), which only the ship of the Argonauts ever escaped.

Choosing to go around the Clashing Rocks, Odysseus then must confront *either* Scylla or Charybdis. The first is a six-headed monster lurking in an overhanging, fog-concealed cavern. She cannot be defeated in battle, and she will devour at least six of the Greeks, one for each of her hideous heads that feature triple rows of thickset fangs. No more than an arrow shot away is Charybdis, a monster whirlpool that swallows everything near it three times a day.

If the Greeks survive these terrors, they will meet the most dangerous test of all: the temptation of the island (Thrinacia) of the Sungod Helios. Whatever they do, the seamen must not harm the sacred cattle of the sun. If they resist temptation, they can return home safely; if, on the other hand, they harm any sacred animal, the ship and men will be destroyed. Odysseus alone may survive, but he will return home late and alone, a broken man. This last caveat (12.148–53) echoes the curse of the Cyclops (9.590–95) and the prophecy of Tiresias (11.125–35). Circe's warnings prove to be a foreshadowing of the true events.

Commentary

Loyalty and keeping promises are two of the highest virtues in Homer's world. Despite the horrors of the Land of the Dead and the relief of escape, Odysseus' first thought is to return to Aeaea to bury Elpenor's corpse. The brief description of the burial rites tells us that the body is burned on a funeral pyre, along with the warrior's armor. The ashes are buried in a mound topped with a monumental stone and the seaman's oar that is "planted . . . to crown his tomb" (12.15). The ceremony is similar to that of the seafaring warriors at the end of the Old English epic *Beowulf*, composed almost 1,500 years later.

Character Insight

Like that of the Lotus-eaters, the section on the Sirens is surprisingly short (fewer than 40 lines), considering that it is one of the best known episodes in the epic. Once again, Homer has touched on a universal truth, mankind's struggle with deadly but irresistible appeal. Circe's solution is realistic and simple: Odysseus' men stop their ears with beeswax. Knowing Odysseus as well as she does, Circe realizes that his intellectual curiosity must be satisfied; he has to hear the Sirens' song. The solution is to lash him to the mast of the ship and, when he pleads to be set free, to tie him more securely. For any man who goes too close to shore, she warns, "no sailing home for him, no wife rising to meet him, / no happy children beaming up at their father's face" (12.48–49). Thus warned and protected, the crew survives temptation, although Odysseus is nearly driven mad by his desire to submit to the Sirens' call.

Character Insight

Getting past Scylla and Charybdis calls for ultimate leadership on the part of Odysseus. Not only must he exercise proper judgment, but he must also recognize that, even if things go well, he still loses six good men. Following Circe's advice, he avoids the whirlpool (Charybdis) and tries the side of the six-headed monster (Scylla). Against his instincts, he pushes through the monster's attack without stopping for a fight, realizing that delay would only cost him more men. He loses the six to a writhing death, the most heart-wrenching experience for Odysseus in all his wanderings.

The final test of judgment in Odysseus' wanderings takes place at the island of Thrinacia, land of the Sungod Helios. Odysseus wants to bypass the island because of Tiresias' prophecy and Circe's warning. However, his men are tired and hungry. In addition, the night sea is especially dangerous. Eurylocus speaks for the crew and begs Odysseus to land on the island so that the men can rest and prepare a proper meal. He assures Odysseus that they have plenty of supplies onboard and that, therefore, Odysseys need not worry about his men raiding the island or harming the sacred cattle. Arguably showing more compassion than leadership, Odysseus gives in.

Initially, the decision seems benign. There *is* plenty of food and drink aboard ship. But for one entire month, the crew is stranded due to a lack of favorable wind. The ship's stores run low. Odysseus goes inland to pray for help from the gods but falls into a deep sleep, just as he did when approaching Ithaca with the ill winds contained in an ox skin pouch. And, as they did on that occasion (10.39 ff.), his men revolt. Led by Eurylochus, they slaughter the finest of the sacred cattle of the Sungod, ironically going through with a sacrificial ceremony, making libations with water because the wine is gone.

The gods are not appeased by the sacrifice, and Zeus himself is outraged but waits for vengeance until the ship sets sail a week later. As soon as land is out of sight, Zeus sends a monstrous storm that destroys the vessel and kills all the men, sparing only Odysseus. Quickly making a raft of the mast and keel, Odysseus survives the vortex of Charybdis and struggles ashore ten days later at Ogygia, the island of Calypso. There he is held captive for the next seven years.

Glossary

Argo   ship of the Argonauts.

Hera   sister and wife of Zeus.

Jason   captain of the *Argo* and leader of the Argonauts in quest of the Golden Fleece; husband of Medea.

lowing   mooing of cattle.

Books 13 & 14
Ithaca at Last; The Loyal Swineherd

Summary

Odysseus' account of his wanderings is complete. The Phaeacians know the rest. They are silent for a few seconds until Alcinous speaks to assure Odysseus that he will be returned safely to his home and to insist on even more gifts for the guest. Odysseus will arrive in Ithaca with treasure surpassing his fair share from Troy, which has long since been lost. Consistent with their custom, the Phaeacians provide the wanderer safe passage home. This annoys Poseidon who complains to Zeus. The gods agree on Poseidon's vengeance against the Phaeacians.

Athena meets Odysseus on Ithaca and disguises him as an old beggar so that he can gain information without being recognized. He meets his loyal swineherd, Eumaeus, and is pleased with the man's hospitality as well as his devotion to his master, whom he does not recognize.

Commentary

The pace slows as the story returns from the fantastic world of the wanderings. These books serve to return Odysseus, at last, to Ithaca; in addition, they further consider two of the most important themes in the epic: hospitality and loyalty.

Theme

One of the controversies in this section of the tale is that the Phaeacians, who are models of hospitality, apparently are to be punished by the gods for their kindness and generosity. Poseidon (13.142–157) complains to Zeus that he is disrespected by the mortals and will lose face with other gods because the Phaeacians have returned Odysseus safely to his homeland. The overriding conflict here is that Poseidon wants to punish the Phaeacians for granting safe passage to wayfaring strangers, a custom that is an exceptional virtue in Homer's world. The situation is further complicated because Zeus is the protector of wayfaring strangers and suppliants. As the introduction to Fagles and Knox puts it (p. 44), "If there is one stable moral criterion in the world of *The Odyssey*, it is the care taken by the powerful and well-to-do of strangers, wanderers and beggars." Zeus turns his back on this ideal code of conduct.

Echoing the prophecy of Alcinous' father, which the son, now King of Phaeacia, mentioned (8.631–641) just before Odysseus began the story of his wanderings, Poseidon vows to crush the ship that carries Odysseus home, sinking it (and all the men aboard) before the vessel can dock safely. Then he'll "pile a huge mountain" (13.173) around the Phaeacian port, ostensibly ending the sailing days of these peaceful, seafaring folk. Adding a touch of sculpture to the plan, Zeus suggests turning the ship to stone within sight of shore and then building the mountain around the harbor.

There are two possible loopholes for the Phaeacians. The first is that Poseidon can always change his mind. When Alcinous first told of the prophecy, he mentioned that the sea god could follow through with the vengeance or leave it undone, "whatever warms his heart" (8.641). As soon as Poseidon turns the ship to stone, the Phaeacians do decide to appease him before he closes their port forever. Alcinous quickly promises to stop the trips home for castaways and calls for the sacrifice of a dozen of the finest bulls in hopes of appeasing Poseidon.

Style & Language

The other hope for the Phaeacians is textual and was first advocated by the ancient editor Aristophanes of Byzantium. He pointed out that a slight alteration in the Greek (changing three letters) has Zeus telling Poseidon to turn the ship to stone but *not* to close the harbor. This interpretation seems more consistent with the rest of the epic and with the reputation of Zeus. Unfortunately, we never find out what happens. Homer leaves the Phaeacians' fate to our imaginations.

Now in Ithaca, Odysseus needs protection. He slept for most of the journey from Phaeacia and is unable to recognize Ithaca when he awakes. Athena has provided a mist to cover the land so that she can privately alter Odysseus' appearance and help him hide his treasure. Athena turns the hero into an old beggar, even going so far as to shrivel his skin, remove the "russet curls" (13.456) from his head, and dim the fire in his eyes. As he did successfully in *The Iliad*, Odysseus poses as a beggar to gather information.

Odysseus' first human contact is with his swineherd, Eumaeus, the epitome of loyalty and hospitality. Eumaeus repeatedly praises his old king but insists that his master must be dead despite the beggar's promise that Odysseus will soon return. Eumaeus despises the suitors. As a keeper of his master's property, he especially resents the way that the louts have diminished the droves of pigs and herds of cattle. He is kind to the apparent wayfaring stranger, and Odysseus is especially pleased with the swineherd.

Glossary

cauldron a large kettle or vat.

Phorcys an old sea god.

King Priam's craggy city Troy; "craggy" refers to a steep incline of rocks, a barrier.

naiads any of several nymphs living in and presiding over bodies of water.

Idomeneus commander of the warriors from Crete at Troy.

Phoenician a person from ancient Phoenicia, a region along the eastern shores of the Mediterranean.

Libya a kingdom in northern Africa.

Cronus a primordial god who ruled the world until dethroned by his son Zeus.

Thesprotia a region in northwestern Greece.

Dulichion island near Ithaca.

Books 15 & 16
The Prince Sets Sail for Home;
Father and Son

Summary

Eumaeus and the beggar/Odysseus continue their conversations, the swineherd proving a perfect host and loyal servant. He tells the story of his life and how he came to Ithaca. Meanwhile, Athena guides Telemachus safely past the suitors' ambush; she tells him to go directly to the pig farm upon arrival at Ithaca. Eumaeus is sent to tell Penelope of her son's safe return. Athena takes this opportunity to alter Odysseus' appearance once more, turning him into a strapping image of his former self; he looks like a god to the shocked and skeptical Telemachus. Odysseus reveals his true identity to his son, and they work out a plan to defeat the suitors.

Meanwhile, Antinous also has a plan and tells the other suitors how they must assassinate the prince. However, Amphinomus, the most decent of the suitors, calls for patience in order to learn the will of the gods before striking. His argument wins the day as the suitors agree to postpone the murder of Telemachus. Penelope confronts the intruders but is cut off by the smooth-talking Eurymachus.

Back at the pig farm, Athena has turned Odysseus back into the old beggar. Among the mortals, only Telemachus knows who he really is.

Commentary

The bond between Odysseus and his swineherd grows as Eumaeus insists that the beggar should stay on at the farm and not take his chances in town with the suitors. The friendship undoubtedly is easier for Homer's audience to accept when Eumaeus tells his life story, revealing that he actually is of royal blood but was kidnapped from his home and eventually purchased as a slave by Odysseus' father, Laertes. While Odysseus is sympathetic and respects his loyal servant, he has no thought of freeing the man. Nor does he reveal his true identity to the swineherd. That revelation is saved for his son.

Theme

As powerful, brave, and worthy as Odysseus is, he needs Athena's help at almost every step during his return to power. At this point, she must get Telemachus past the suitors' ambush and out to the pig farm with Odysseus so that they can become partners in revenge. Athena accomplishes this by guiding the prince around the planned area of attack and instructing him to leave the ship early and go directly to Eumaeus' hut. After Telemachus' arrival, Eumaeus is sent to Penelope with the news of her son's safe return. Father and son are left alone. Taking Odysseus aside, Athena performs another transformation, returning him to an impressive image of his former self. Appearing in a form that Odysseus can see but Telemachus can't, Athena counsels the king on when and how to reveal his true identity.

Character Insight

As a beggar, Odysseus has already dared to challenge his son about the suitors. He asks how the prince can tolerate them. Telemachus may not have learned much about his father's presence during the trips to Pylos and Sparta, but he has gained considerable maturity and insight. He listens to the beggar and agrees that he must stand up to the scoundrels who have taken over his home. So when Odysseus identifies himself to his son, Odysseus knows that he has a willing and increasingly able partner. Being the experienced warrior that he is, Odysseus seeks reliable information about the enemy. His first step is to ask Telemachus about the suitors.

The prince reveals (16.270–287) that there are some 108 noblemen, plus assorted servants and one bard (Medon), in the group and wonders how the two of them can overcome such numbers. Odysseus puts his faith in Athena and Zeus. With that as a premise, the father and son devise their plan. Telemachus is to return to town and mix with the suitors. Odysseus, in disguise, will follow. No matter how poorly the suitors may treat the old beggar, Odysseus and Telemachus are to bide their time and refrain from striking back until the moment is right. At a signal, the prince is to gather all the weapons and place them in the storeroom. If challenged, he can say that he does this to protect the gear. He must leave out weapons only for himself and his father.

Antinous is the most aggressive of the suitors. Concerned that public opinion is shifting to the side of the prince, he wants to strike immediately, assassinating Telemachus before he can gather support. The suitors, especially Antinous, are haughty and arrogant, which prove to be their downfall. This outspoken leader's arrogant plan includes seizing all of Telemachus' land and valuables immediately after the murder and dispensing them among the freeloaders. The palace itself will go to Penelope and, of course, the man she weds—a man Antinous believes to be himself.

Only Amphinomus has the courage to speak against the plot. He is the most decent of the suitors and Penelope's favorite because he usually demonstrates good sense and refinement. Amphinomus points out that killing nobility is nasty business and suggests that they hold off on the assassination to see whether the gods have some bias in the matter. The rest of the suitors, most of whom are cowards, gladly accept this reprieve. Lacking the support he needs, Antinous must abandon his plot.

The speeches by Antinous, Eurymachus, and Amphinomus clearly delineate their characters. When Penelope confronts the suitors' about their rancor toward her son, Eurymachus typically tries to finesse the situation with smooth talk. He is a manipulator and a liar, the kind of fellow who thinks that he is much smarter than he is. When he claims, "So to *me* your son is the dearest man alive" (16.493), Penelope is not fooled. She is, nonetheless, still alone and vulnerable. She cries herself to sleep that night, longing for Odysseus. What she does not know is that he is nearby.

Glossary

Same island near Ithaca.

Elis a region in the northwestern Peloponnesus near Pylos.

Ctimene Odysseus' younger sister.

Ortygia island where Artemis killed Orion.

Artemis virgin goddess of the hunt and moon, twin sister of Apollo.

Zacynthus an island in Odysseus' kingdom, south of Ithaca.

in your cups drunk, inebriated.

Book 17
Stranger at the Gate

Summary

Odysseus walks to town the next morning, joined by Eumaeus, who still thinks he is accompanying an old beggar. Telemachus precedes them, cheering his mother with his presence and the stories of his trip. With the prince is a seer, Theoclymenus, who tells Penelope that Odysseus is on Ithaca *now*, gathering information. The queen wishes that she could believe him, but she cannot.

During the trip to town, Odysseus and his swineherd cross paths with a bully, the goatherd Melanthius, but avoid a fight. In one famously poignant moment, Odysseus and his dying old dog, Argos, quietly recognize each other. In the banquet hall, Antinous bullies the ragged beggar/Odysseus and even throws a footstool at him. Exercising considerable restraint, both the king and his son manage to postpone revenge.

Commentary

Theme

Judgment and prudence are the dominating heroic characteristics developed in this chapter. When Telemachus visits his mother, he very much wants to put her mind at ease; but he dares not reveal that his father has, in fact, returned. He details the encouraging news from Menelaus, King of Sparta, that Odysseus was captive but alive on Calypso's island. He encourages Theoclymenus' report that the king lives and is now on Ithaca. At this point, though, prudence stops him from revealing to anyone—including his mother—that Odysseus is home and preparing to strike. Penelope, who has heard rumors and listened to prophecies for years, would like to believe Theoclymenus, but prudence does not allow her to.

Odysseus must exercise restraint on several occasions. On their way to town, he and Eumaeus are confronted by Melanthius, a bully and braggart who is in Odysseus' employ as a goatherd. The bully verbally assaults the two travelers and even kicks Odysseus as he passes. Odysseus is tempted to split the lout's head on a rock but controls himself. Eumaeus steps in and defends the beggar/Odysseus. This faithful swineherd is the antithesis of Melanthius. Where one is considerate, kind, refined, and loyal, the other is impudent, cruel, crude, and appeasing toward the suitors. Odysseus exercises the judgment of a sage when he refrains from dispatching Melanthius on the spot.

A more subtle restraint is necessary soon after that confrontation. As Odysseus and his swineherd approach the palace, they spot a pathetic, old, tick-infested dog, "half-dead from neglect" (17.328), lying on a dung pile. It is Argos, the king's pet as a pup, now some 20 years old. The dog recognizes his master, thumps his tail, but is too weak to move toward him. Odysseus, too, recognizes his dog but knows he cannot show it. He turns away to hide a tear as the old dog dies.

At the great hall of the palace, Odysseus has more need for judgment, prudence, and restraint. The suitors are feasting well on the best of Odysseus' sheep, hogs, fatted goats, and cattle. Telemachus, aided by Athena (who is always near during this crucial period), encourages the beggar/Odysseus to make the rounds of the young noblemen and ask for handouts. Most of the suitors give him something, a scrap or crust. But Antinous, reminiscent of the ill-mannered goatherd on the road into town, verbally assaults Eumaeus and sardonically challenges the swineherd's decision to bring such a despicable old vagabond (Odysseus) to interrupt his dining. Eumaeus risks his own life by talking back to Antinous, but Telemachus wisely intercedes and directs the debate toward himself.

The truth is, of course, that the food is Odysseus' to begin with. More than a little perturbed, but staying in character as an old beggar, he pointedly asks Antinous for a "crust" in words that have double meaning; they sound flattering but are actually insulting. He jabs at the reason for Antinous' presence by saying, "You look like a king to me!" (17.460) Odysseus doesn't slacken his caustic remarks, and Antinous becomes increasingly angry, finally hurling a footstool at the beggar and striking him in the back.

Odysseus foreshadows the showdown in Book 22 by wishing that Antinous might "meet his death before he meets his bride!" (17.525), but he does not strike back. Prudence prevails. The king and his son stop short of violence, although it is especially difficult for Telemachus to see his father treated so. The feast resumes, but Antinous has sealed his fate with his rude arrogance. The suitors will be given more opportunities to atone for their actions, but Athena (17.399) has already decided to kill them all.

Penelope notices the beggar/Odysseus and asks Eumaeus about him. The swineherd tells how impressed he was during his three days with the visitor, and Penelope requests that the guest speak with her. Feigning anxiety about the suitors, Odysseus says he will meet with her but prefers to wait until later.

The tone here is threatening and ominous. There is a dramatic increase of tension from the time that Odysseus arrives at the palace until the showdown in Book 22. Like the goatherd on the road, the suitors doom themselves with their crude arrogance. Even those who seem not particularly disagreeable, like Amphinomus, are guilty by their complicity and acquiescence. They will have their opportunities to leave but will choose to stay. That's enough for Athena. Dusk is falling fast on the suitors.

Glossary

Apollo god of archery and patron of the arts.

Nile a major river in Egypt, extending into other parts of eastern Africa.

Cyprus an island in the Mediterranean off southern Turkey.

Thesprotia a region in northwestern Greece.

Book 18
The Beggar-King at Ithaca

Summary

As late afternoon turns to evening, another vagabond, named Irus, arrives. He is a portly buffoon who is a comic favorite of the suitors. At the urging of Antinous, Irus picks a fight with beggar/Odysseus, which he soon regrets. As tensions increase, Odysseus tries in vain to warn Amphinomus, the best of the suitors, that trouble is coming and he should leave the group.

In preparation for the meeting with Odysseus, Athena makes Penelope look even more beautiful. The queen chastises her son for permitting a fight and putting their guest at risk.

Odysseus rebukes Penelope's maidservant Melantho for her neglect of the queen. The impudent girl has been indulging in an illicit affair with Eurymachus, Penelope's smooth-talking suitor. Odysseus and Eurymachus have a confrontation.

Commentary

Literary Device

Some critics see the fight between Odysseus and Irus as comic relief, but it is hardly a laughing matter for anyone other than the pernicious suitors. Although a buffoon and braggart, Irus is a pathetic figure. Irus' character mirrors that of Antinous: Both are insolent bullies. Nonetheless, Antinous is considerably more dangerous because he has power, prestige, and intelligence. Irus is little more than a servant for the suitors. He is a mock champion, a sad joke, a fake. Although the old clown annoys Odysseus, Odysseus doesn't really want to hurt him. He breaks the vagrant's jaw more by reflex than design. Odysseus does display his impressive physique for the tussle, and the incident foreshadows later triumphs.

At this point, Athena is more set on complete revenge than is Odysseus. The king is especially concerned for suitor Amphinomus, the best of the bunch and Penelope's favorite. He tries in vain to persuade Amphinomus that Penelope's vengeful husband is "right at hand" (18.167) and that he must get out while he can.

Theme

The theme of loyalty appears again when Odysseus rebukes Melantho, primarily because the maidservant is ignoring her queen's needs. She is also spending her nights with Eurymachus. The latter is known for his smooth talk, but he loses control when Odysseus stands up to him. He throws a stool at the beggar/Odysseus but hits the wine steward instead. At this point, Telemachus, backed by Amphinomus, calls an end to the evening's revels.

Glossary

Echetus a mainland Greek king known for his cruelty.

Ionian refers to people of the northeastern Peloponnesus.

Argos here, a region in the northeastern Peloponnesus.

Book 19
Penelope and Her Guest

Summary

The suitors have gone home for the night. Odysseus instructs Telemachus to gather the weapons and hide them where they will not be readily available to the suitors the next day. Melantho, the disrespectful servant girl who sleeps with Eurymachus, confronts the beggar/Odysseus once more.

Finally alone with Penelope, Odysseus offers convincing evidence that he knew her husband. Penelope seems suspicious about his identity. An old nurse, Eurycleia, is assigned the duty of bathing the guest. She innocently comments on how much he resembles her king, whom she raised from early childhood. Stunned, she identifies a scar, over his knee, left by a boar's tusk, and realizes that she is, indeed, bathing, her master. Odysseus immediately and sternly swears her to silence, forbidding her even to tell Penelope his identity.

After the bath, Penelope rejoins the beggar/Odysseus and reveals that she will conduct a contest the following day to select a husband and satisfy the suitors. The challenge involves a feat that only Odysseus has performed before: stringing his great bow and shooting an arrow through a straight row of twelve axes. Odysseus enthusiastically approves of her plan.

Commentary

Character Insight

This section of the epic is primarily concerned with the question of Odysseus' identity. Scholars disagree vehemently on how much Penelope knows. On the surface, she seems to accept the beggar as another wayfaring stranger, certainly more interesting than most but of no great personal significance to her. The beggar/Odysseus repeatedly states that her husband's return is imminent; she remains skeptical. Beneath the surface, however, the reader can see several indications that Penelope is at least suspicious about the vagrant's true identity.

When Odysseus and Penelope finally meet, she directs the conversation. First she wants the beggar/Odysseys to understand her considerable efforts to dissuade the suitors: She has used her son's youth as an excuse. For three years, she held the suitors off through her ruse of the shroud, telling the suitors that she must finish a shroud for Laertes, her father-in-law, against that sad but inevitable time of his death. During the day, she worked at her loom in view of the suitors; at night, she unraveled the day's weaving. She was successful in this deception until her own maidservant revealed the truth, a point that also influences Odysseus' eventual judgment of the servants in Book 22.

Having in this way identified herself to the visitor, Penelope probes him for information about his background. Odysseus answers with a fictitious autobiography that includes a friendship with her husband. Penelope tests him by asking specific questions about the clothing and comrades of Odysseus. The beggar/Odysseus has impressive answers, citing a purple woolen cape and a gold clasp with a hound clenching a fawn. He mentions Odysseus' herald, Eurybates. Finally, he predicts that her husband will return as the old moon dies and a new moon rises that very month. (Critics mention this as one of several references to death and rebirth in the epic, other references being Odysseus' return from the Land of the Dead; his arrival, naked and caked with mud, on Phaeacia; and his return to Ithaca.) Penelope concedes the accuracy of the description of her husband but wonders, momentarily and beautifully, if he ever really existed: "Odysseus. There was a man, or was he all a dream?" (19.363)

Style & Language

The strongest case for concluding that Penelope is at least suspicious that the stranger is her husband begins with her call to Eurycleia to bathe the guest. She tells the nurse to "come and wash your master's . . . equal in years" (19.407). Penelope seems to have started to ask the nurse to wash her master's feet. She changes this, mid-sentence, to an unlikely phrase about the guest's being the master's *age*. Translator Fagles uses an ellipsis to indicate a pause, effected by word order in the Greek. Eurycleia, who cared for Odysseus when he was a boy, soon identifies him as her master (in large part because of the scar above his knee, which she sees while bathing him).

Further supporting the assumption that Penelope is aware of the beggar's identity is that, following the bath, she confides in him to a remarkable degree. She shares a dream with him, in which an eagle kills her flock of geese and then takes on a human voice to tell her that he, the eagle, is her husband and the geese are the suitors. Penelope wonders if this is a dream from the gate of ivory (meaning that it is insignificant) or the gate of horn (indicating that the dream is true or prophetic).

Most interesting is the contest that Penelope decides will choose her husband. The test, the next day, will be to see who can properly string Odysseus' great bow and shoot a single arrow cleanly through a dozen axes set in a row. Surely it is no accident that only one man, Odysseus himself, has ever been able to perform this feat.

Glossary

Icmalius a chair maker and wood craftsman on Ithaca.

shroud a cloth, often ornate, used to wrap a body for burial.

Cnossos a major city on Crete.

Parnassus a peak (about 8,060 feet high) in southern Greece, north of the Gulf of Corinth.

Book 20
Portents Gather

Summary

Odysseus spends a restless night worrying about the impending battle. He angrily notices the maidservants as they sneak out to meet their lovers among the suitors. Suddenly Athena appears and assures him of vengeful victory. Penelope's room is nearby, and at dawn, he hears the end of her prayer for death if she cannot join her husband. He imagines (20.105) that she recognizes him and that they are together at last. Odysseus prays to Zeus for a sign of support and is answered by a thunderclap.

This day is a special holiday on Ithaca, a festal celebration in honor of Apollo, god of archery. Melanthius, the goatherd, is in town for the celebration and again bullies Odysseus. Eumaeus, the swineherd, continues to earn his master's trust as does Philoetius, a cowherd. The suitors, talking again of assassinating Telemachus, continue their boorish behavior. One of the lot, Ctesippus, mocks beggar/Odysseus and hurls an oxhoof at the king. Telemachus berates the suitors and lists some of their many offenses. The seer Theoclymenus speaks ominously to them, offering one of their last warnings, but in their arrogance, the suitors respond with derisive laughter.

Commentary

As the hour of the battle approaches, the tone is ominous. Evidence mounts against the suitors. Odysseus is, wisely, uneasy while the suitors go blithely about their usual proceedings, failing to notice the gathering storm.

Theme

Homer devotes much of this section to a collection of evidence against the maidservants and suitors. Odysseus hears the maids as they sneak out of the house, giggling in anticipation of another night with their lovers. Their trysts with the suitors especially bother him because these are blatant acts of disloyalty toward Penelope. The goatherd Melanthius is another disloyal servant. We remember him from his assault on the beggar/Odysseus during the king's initial trip to town with Eumaeus. Melanthius again bullies the guest. The suitors behave in their usual haughty manner. Ctesippus takes his turn insulting the disguised king and casts an oxhoof at him. Further building the case against the suitors, Telemachus boldly scolds them and catalogues their offenses. Although Telemachus may be emboldened partly because he is aware of his father's presence, this passage also demonstrates that he is now a stronger, more mature prince than the one portrayed early in the epic. He is ready for his first real battle. The effect of this detail, as well as Telemachus' recitation of the suitors' many violations is to further justify the merciless revenge that is about to take place.

Theme

Preparation for battle must include intervention by the gods. Athena comes to Odysseus in the night and guarantees success even if he were to face "fifty bands of mortal fighters" (20.53), and Zeus, responding to Odysseus' request for a sign, produces a massive roll of thunder. Penelope, too, hopes for help from the gods and asks that she die if she cannot be with her husband. Finally, Penelope has chosen Apollo the Archer's celebration for the contest of the bow. Not only is the contest fitting for archers, but Apollo's arrows carry death—as will those of Odysseus this day.

The suitors have been repeatedly warned, individually and as a group. Their standard response is to mock the speaker. Evidence has been gathered. In effect, they have testified against themselves. The gods have condemned the intruders. Justice, like a terrible storm, is about to break upon them.

Glossary

Pandareus father of the nightingale. See Fagles and Knox (pp. 514–515) for a thorough consideration.

the distant deadly Archer Apollo.

charlatan an impostor, fraud or fake.

Book 21
Odysseus Strings His Bow

Summary

Penelope announces the contest and retrieves Odysseus' great back-sprung bow from a secret storeroom deep in the palace. For sport, Telemachus attempts to string the bow and fails three times. He is about to succeed on his fourth try when Odysseus privately signals him to back off. The suitors then take their turns, their early efforts failing dismally. As the suitors contend, Odysseus meets outside with Eumaeus and Philoetius, his faithful servants and reveals to them his true identity and enlists their support in his plan.

Meanwhile, the suitors continue to struggle with the bow. Antinous suggests that the contest be postponed until the next day, but then Odysseus asks if he might give the bow a try, an idea that Penelope strongly supports. Odysseus easily strings the weapon and fires an arrow straight through the axes; then he and Telemachus stand together to face the suitors.

Commentary

Character Insight

Penelope's choice of contest—one that only Odysseus could win—supports the suspicion that she is aware of the beggar/Odysseus's real identity. When the beggar/Odysseus asks for an unofficial chance at the bow, Penelope immediately counters Antinous' objection. Dismissing the idea that the guest would claim her as his bride, she responds that by giving the wandering stranger a shot she is simply being hospitable. Of course, the beggar would not claim her for his bride; Odysseus would not have to.

Scholars have long pondered the details of the contest itself, the most debatable point being what shooting an arrow through a dozen axes actually means. Fagles and Knox's offer this solution (p. 515): Each ax has its handle attached. Each handle probably has a metal ring on the end opposite the blade so that it can easily be hung on a wall peg. That ring is what Odysseus shoots his arrow through. Twelve in a row is an amazing but conceivable feat, and because he is sitting on a stool at the time, he is at about the right height for such a shot.

Literary Device

Several folklore motifs appear in this section of the epic. Most prominent is a contest involving a mystical weapon that only the hero can wield. In *Beowulf*, for example, the hero (Beowulf) strikes down his foe's (Grendel's) mother with a mystical sword inscribed with runic symbols. In the Arthurian legend, only Arthur, the true king, is able to pull the sword Excalibur from the stone. The difference here is that the challenge in *The Odyssey* requires less magic and more skill and physical strength. Other motifs are the disguise of the hero, the battle for the bride, revenge upon interlopers, maturation of the heir apparent, and restoration of a king to his rightful reign.

Character Insight

Telemachus' role at the contest is secondary but significant. His attempt at stringing the bow symbolically illustrates that, although he isn't quite yet ready to assume the burden of leadership from Odysseus, he is, indeed, the destined heir to Odysseus' legacy. Some critics also complain that Telemachus is unduly rude when he sends his mother to her quarters as Odysseus is about to string the bow; other suggest that he is angry. Neither is the case. In fact, Telemachus is accomplishing two important tasks. He is asserting his own position in the household, and he is removing his mother from harm's way. She may suspect that the beggar is her husband, but Telemachus *knows* that a battle is about to take place and that his place is at the side of the king.

Style & Language

The structure of the contest section is especially effective. First Penelope introduces the idea, which is news to the suitors. Antinous immediately feels threatened. He attacks his underlings, Eumaeus and Philoetius, a safe way for him to let out aggression. Then he hypocritically praises Odysseus, the king he otherwise mocks and hopes to replace. The purpose of this passage is not just to advance the plot. Here, the reader is given important insights into the characters by virtue of Homer's arrangement of the events. Homer shifts the reader's focus as a film director might.

After the contest gets underway, Homer cleverly takes the reader outside the great hall to a scene in which Odysseus identifies himself and shows his famous scar to his loyal servants, Eumaeus and Philoetius. Then he asks the former to get the maidservants out of the hall and the latter to bolt the courtyard's outer gate. In addition to enabling Odysseus to recruit the help of two faithful servants, this passage also spares the reader the boring task of watching suitor after suitor fail to string the bow.

Style & Language

The whole energy of the section seems to be dying when Antinous successfully requests a postponement of the contest, but Odysseus revitalizes it by asking for a chance at the bow. Antinous immediately objects. Penelope counters. Telemachus intercedes and takes over. Just as the action hits this staccato beat, Odysseus slows it down, teases the onlookers by toying with the bow, and then . . . and then . . . easily strings it and casually shoots the arrow through the axes. Zeus accentuates the action with a thunderbolt, in essence indicating that something important has just been accomplished and something more important is about to take place.

Glossary

Messene a city in Menelaus' kingdom of Lacedaemon in the southern Peloponnesus.

Mycenae Agamemnon's capital city.

Centaur a mythological creature that is part man, part horse.

Book 22
Slaughter in the Hall

Summary

Tearing off his beggar rags, Odysseus boldly catapults himself onto the hall's threshold, utters a brief prayer to Apollo, and fires an arrow straight through a new target: Antinous' throat. Only after that does he announce his intentions to the suitors in no uncertain terms. Suddenly realizing the danger, Eurymachus tries to talk his way out of the situation, offering repayment for all that has been taken from Odysseus. The king declines the offer, and Eurymachus calls his cohorts to arms, which consist of only the swords they wear. They have no armor. Odysseus rips through Eurymachus' chest and liver with an arrow. Amphinomus attacks and is killed by Telemachus. The battle is on.

Goatherd Melanthius, who twice assaulted Odysseus in recent days, manages to bring the suitors armor and spears from the storeroom but is caught by Eumaeus and Philoetius on a second attempt and strung up, alive, to be dealt with later. With Athena's intervention and encouragement, Odysseus wins the day. All suitors are killed. The king then dispenses justice to a few remaining individuals and a dozen servant girls.

Commentary

Character Insight

Odysseus' judgment and prudence finally pay off. Like the superb military leader that he is, he has assessed the situation, devised an effective plan, and implemented it at just the right moment. Although his anger is obvious, he is completely under control. Odysseus kills the enemy's most aggressive leader, Antinous, before any of the suitors realize that the king has returned or that they are in danger. With the leader dead, confusion races through the crowd.

Eurymachus, typically, tries to talk his way out of the situation. He claims that everything was Antinous' fault; the rest were simply under his control and now are prepared to serve their king. He offers to tax the people to pay back everything and adds that he and the other suitors will contribute plenty of their own possessions as well. Odysseus, however, is interested in only one kind of repayment. Eurymachus sees that he must fight or die and calls his fellow suitors to arms. He barely mounts a charge before the king's arrow rips through his chest and into his liver.

Even the relatively good must die. Amphinomus charges. Although he is the queen's favorite and the one suitor whom Odysseus earlier tried to persuade to leave, he is killed by Telemachus.

Because of his military expertise, the early battle goes well for Odysseus. He has caught the enemy by surprise, cut off escape, destroyed its leadership, and caused confusion. Telemachus fetches armor for the king and himself as well as the two loyal herdsmen. The suitors have only the swords that they wear. However, the sinister goatherd Melanthius complicates matters. Familiar with the castle, he retrieves a dozen spears and armor to match from the storeroom whose door Telemachus has carelessly left ajar. Odysseus sees the danger but resists panic. His faithful herdsmen cut off Melanthius' second trip and hang him live by the rafters.

At this crucial point in the battle, as Odysseus agonizes, Athena appears in the form of Mentor. The king recognizes his true mentor, the goddess, and takes heart as she reminds him that these are *not* Trojans that he faces. These are only the suitors. He fights on with renewed vigor. A highlight occurs when Philoetius, the cowherd, rips a spear through the chest of Ctesippus, the braggart who threw an oxhoof at beggar/Odysseus. The king's faithful servant can't resist asking Ctesippus how he likes his mockery now (22.301).

Odysseus dispenses justice harshly but not without mercy. Leodes pleads that he was only the suitors' priest, but Odysseus knows that he was the first to try to string the bow and win Penelope. Odysseus decapitates him with one swipe, the head softly bouncing in the dust. Following Telemachus' recommendation, the king spares Phemius the bard and one of the heralds.

With classic understatement, Odysseus observes that he has only a few "household chores" (22.400) left to tend to. He asks Eurycleia to identify the maidservants who were disloyal. A dozen are called in. They must clean the gore from the great hall, after which they are taken to the courtyard and hanged. The maidservants "kicked up heels for a little—not for long" (22.500). Then Melanthius, the goatherd who assaulted Odysseus on the road to town and later mocked him at the palace, is dragged into the courtyard. His nose and ears are cut off. His genitals are torn from his groin and fed to the dogs. His hands and feet are severed. It is safe to assume that he dies.

Style & Language

The detailed descriptions of the battle and executions are especially effective, realistic, and thorough. The accounts of the deaths of Antinous (22.8–21) and Eurymachus (22.87–93) set the tone for the battle. The description of the deaths of the servant girls, who are compared to "doves or thrushes beating their spread wings / against some snare rigged up in thickets" (22.494–95) has a macabre beauty. What we come away with is this: In this land which has no courts or police and where each must settle his own disputes, Odysseus is not a man to offend.

The house is fumigated, probably with sulfur, for purposes both practical and symbolic. Odysseus' long struggle is over. The enemy is vanquished. His house is finally cleansed. It is time to reunite with Penelope.

Glossary

buckler a small, usually round shield that is carried or worn on the arm or shoulder.

smoke ducts openings high on the walls to allow smoke to escape.

javelin a light spear designed for throwing.

Sungod Helios.

Book 23
The Great Rooted Bed

Summary

Now that the battle has ended and the house has been cleaned, good nurse Eurycleia scurries up to Penelope's quarters to tell her all that has happened. As much as Penelope would like to believe that her husband has returned and vanquished the suitors, she is cautious and goes to the great hall to see for herself. When she expresses ambivalence, Telemachus chides his mother for her skepticism. Odysseus gently suggests that the prince leave his parents to work things out. He also wants Telemachus to gather the servants and the bard and stage a fake wedding feast so that any passersby do not suspect the slaughter that has taken place.

To assure herself of Odysseus' identity, Penelope tests him. As he listens, she asks Eurycleia to move the bedstead out of the couple's chamber and spread it with blankets. The king himself had carved the bed as a young man, shaping it out of a living olive tree that grew in the courtyard of the palace. He built the bedroom around the tree and would know that the bed cannot be moved. When Odysseus becomes upset that the original bed may have been destroyed, Penelope is relieved and accepts him as her long-absent husband. For the first time in 20 years, they spend a blissful night together. Athena delays the dawn to grant the couple more time.

Commentary

Character Insight

Although she seems to suspect that the visitor might be her husband, it is not surprising that Penelope is cautious. She has been approached by frauds before. Some critics suggest that the queen's hesitance is feigned, that she knows the visitor is her husband, and that she is simply being coy, perhaps to impress him with her prudence. This interpretation is a stretch beyond the text. Homer depicts a woman who is very hopeful but careful. It is in Penelope's character to test the man one more time to be certain. No outsider would be likely to know the history of the couple's wedding bed, and that final piece of evidence convinces Penelope and liberates her at last.

Odysseus demonstrates the wisdom of an understanding father as well as caution in his treatment of Telemachus. Rather than scolding the son for chiding his mother, Odysseus assures him that the parents will work things out. Still a military strategist, Odysseus knows that the intruders belong to some of the most influential families in the area who will be bent on revenge. He, therefore, asks his son to create the illusion of a wedding feast in the great hall so that anyone passing by will think that one of the suitors has succeeded and not suspect that they have been slaughtered. Giving Telemachus this assignment not only gives Odysseus time alone with Penelope, but it also demonstrates his faith in the maturing prince.

A few responsibilities remain. Odysseus must visit his father, Laertes, who has suffered emotionally from his son's long absence; the families of the suitors will have to be dealt with to avoid civil war; and, sometime, Odysseus must fulfill the prophecy of Tiresias, spoken at the Land of the Dead: The king must walk inland, from a foreign shore, carrying a well-planed oar until he finds people who know nothing of the sea. When someone mistakes the oar for a fan that winnows grain, Odysseus is to plant the oar and sacrifice a ram, a bull, and a wild boar to Poseidon. He can then return home, make offerings to the gods, and live out a peaceful life.

Glossary

tunic a loose, gownlike garment, sleeved or sleeveless, hanging to the knees and worn by men as well as women.

hallmark a stamp of genuineness or excellence.

Helen of Argos the same Helen whose abduction from Sparta brought on the Trojan War. By the time of *The Odyssey*, she is the somewhat matronly queen of Sparta and content to be the wife of King Menelaus.

winnow grain to separate the chaff from wheat or other grain, by tossing it and allowing the wind to blow the chaff away.

Book 24
Peace

Summary

The final book opens with Hermes, the traditional guide, leading the souls of the dead suitors to the Land of the Dead (commonly referred to as *Hades*). These souls pass such Greek heroes as Achilles and Agamemnon. One of the suitors recites the story of the courtship of Penelope, her resistance to the suitors, and Odysseus' revenge.

Back on Ithaca, Odysseus arrives at his father's farm and approaches Laertes, who looks and acts more like a slave than a former king. After identifying himself, Odysseus joins Laertes, Telemachus, and the two faithful herdsmen for a homecoming meal.

Meanwhile, rumor of the slaughter has spread through the city, and Eupithes, father of Antinous (the aggressive leader of the suitors), calls for revenge. More than half of the men follow Eupithes to Laertes' farm, seeking Odysseus and vengeance. Only the intervention of Athena, again appearing as Mentor, avoids another major battle and perhaps civil war.

Commentary

Since classical times, the legitimacy of this final section has been controversial. Some scholars maintain that a later, inferior poet wrote it. They suggest that the epic should end when Odysseus and Penelope reunite. (For a thorough discussion of the issue, see Fagles and Knox, pp. 59–64.) The consensus of opinion, however, is that the last book does belong. It ties up at least three loose ends.

The scene in the Land of the Dead may seem tedious, even intrusive, to modern readers; but it serves to complete the Agamemnon parallel. Agamemnon's ghost celebrates Penelope's fidelity and compares her favorably to his treacherous wife, Clytemnestra (24.210–23). The retelling of Penelope's story and Odysseus' revenge may be better understood if we remember that the epic was presented orally, probably over a period of several days or even weeks. As the rhapsode (a bard specializing in epics) is about to conclude his performance, this interlude updates the audience and anticipates the conclusion.

More germane to the continuing action is the meeting between Odysseus and his father, Laertes. During his visit to the Land of the Dead (Book 11), Odysseus learns from his mother, Anticleia, that old King Laertes suffered greatly from his son's absence. Athena and Eumaeus have also mentioned Laertes' struggle. A serious gap would remain if Odysseus did not reunite with his father and restore him to dignity.

One major problem remains. Odysseus has slaughtered more than 100 young men from powerful families on Ithaca and surrounding islands. He knows that he has to deal with an attempt at revenge, which he earlier mentioned to Athena and postponed by having Telemachus stage a fake wedding feast at the palace the night of the slaughter. Now, Eupithes (father of the chief suitor, Antinous) leads a large contingent in an assault on Laertes' farm. Once again, the gods intervene. The two sides engage in battle. Strengthened by his son's return and Athena's blessing, Laertes kills Eupithes. With one father defeating the other, the war ends there. Under directions from Zeus, Athena stops the conflict and calls for peace and cooperation. Prosperity is restored to Ithaca, and Odysseus is home at last.

Glossary

Thetis a sea goddess, the mother of Achilles.

Nestor ruler of Pylos and eldest of the Greek leaders.

Old Man of the Sea Proteus the shape-shifter, servant of Poseidon.

Dionysus god of wine for whom a cult is named, celebrating the power and fertility of nature.

Cephallenians Fagles and Knox (p. 525) point out that the term is used to refer to all of Odysseus' subjects, but specifically residents of an island west of Ithaca that is part of his kingdom.

CHARACTER ANALYSES

Odysseus

Odysseus is a combination of the self-made, self-assured man and the embodiment of the standards and mores of his culture. He is favored by the gods and respected and admired by the mortals. Even the wrath of Poseidon does not keep him from his homecoming. He is confident that he represents virtue even when a modern audience might not be so sure. He is also a living series of contradictions, a much more complicated character than we would expect to find in the stereotypical epic hero. We can contrast Odysseus, for example, with the great warrior Achilles in *The Iliad*.

Achilles himself is not a two-dimensional stereotype. He has a tragic flaw, which can best be identified as *hubris* (an overbearing arrogance or misguided pride) as one of several distinguishing traits. But Achilles is a simpler character. According to the myth the Homeric Greeks would have known, Achilles was given a choice by the gods to live a short, glorious life full of excitement and heroism or a long, tranquil life with little recognition or fame. Achilles, of course, chose the glorious life; therefore, he achieves a kind of immortality through valor and intense, honest devotion to a cause.

Odysseus, in *The Odyssey*, is much more complicated. He lives by his wiles as well as his courage. He is an intellectual. Often he openly evaluates a situation, demonstrating the logic he employs in making his choices. When it proves effective, Odysseus lies (even to his own family), cheats, or steals in ways that we would not expect in an epic hero. Although he is self-disciplined (refusing to eat the lotus), his curiosity is sometimes the root of his trouble (as with the Cyclops). He is willing to pay a price for knowledge; for example, he insists on hearing the Sirens' call, even though to do so, he must have himself excruciatingly strapped to the mast of his ship so that he cannot give in to the temptation. Odysseus can be merciful, as when he spares the bard Phemius, or brutal, as he seems when dealing with the dozen disloyal maidservants. He creates his own code of conduct through his adventures. He is deeper than Achilles, more contemplative, but still capable of explosive violence; he is almost certainly more interesting. It is easy to see why some critics like to call him the first "modern man."

Victory motivates Odysseus. He wants to return home and live well in Ithaca; as a result, every step along the way is another test, sometimes, another battle. His concern with victory is also cultural, as well as practical. In Homer's world, where there are no police or justice systems, might usually makes right. The strong prevail. Odysseus often has only two choices: death or victory. Even when Athena intervenes on his behalf, she often leaves ultimate success or failure up to Odysseus. During the battle with the suitors, for example, she could easily and quickly prevail; but she makes Odysseus earn the victory.

Appropriately, Odysseus' development as a character is complicated. He is, in every way, "the man of twists and turns" (1.1). While he does seem to grow throughout his wanderings, the reader should not look at each event as a one more learning experience for the hero. *The Odyssey* is not a lesson plan for growth; the episodes are not didactic examples of the importance of prudence or anything else. When Odysseus left for Troy, he had already established his reputation as a hero. His participation in the war was crucial to the Greeks' victory. It was he who disguised himself as an old beggar and infiltrated the enemy. As Menelaus tells Telemachus in Book 4, it was Odysseus' legendary ruse of the Trojan horse that led to the defeat of Troy.

Certainly Odysseus does grow in wisdom and judgment throughout his ventures. His self-control while dealing with the suitors' insults is exemplary and contrasts, for example, with his earlier irresistible urge to announce his name to the Cyclops in Book 9. In other ways, however, he seems slow to learn. The most notable example being his difficulty in controlling his men. After the victory over the Cicones, Odysseus wisely wants to take the plunder and depart quickly (9.50). His men prefer to stay, leading to a defeat at the hands of reinforcements. When Aeolus grants the Greeks fair winds to Ithaca, Odysseus falls asleep within sight of home, enabling his suspicious, undisciplined crew to open the bag of ill winds and let loose a tempest that blows them off course. Again, on the island of the Sungod Helios, Odysseus' men disobey strict orders and feast on the sacred cattle when he goes inland to pray and falls asleep. The struggles Odysseus faces make his growth as a character more realistic and more credible because it is not simple or absolute.

Penelope

Some critics dismiss Penelope as a paragon of marital fidelity—a serious and industrious character, a devoted wife and mother, but one who lacks the fascination and zest for life that some of Homer's *immortal* women display. However, Penelope is not a pasteboard figure. She is a complicated woman with a wiy sense of destiny who weaves her plots as deftly as she weaves a garment.

Penelope is in a very dangerous situation when the suitors begin invading her house and asking—and then demanding—her hand in marriage. Although the suitors abuse an important social tradition of hospitality, Penelope lacks the natural, social, and familial protections that would enable her to remove them from her house. Her son, Telemachus, has neither the maturity nor the strength to expel the invaders. Although unassuming, Penelope has a cunning that indicates she is a good mate for her wily husband. Antinous complains of it at the assembly in Book 2. He claims—rightly, by the way—that she has misguided the suitors for nearly four years, leading on each man with hints and promises but choosing no one.

The story of the loom symbolizes the queen's clever tactics. For three years, Penelope worked at weaving a shroud for the eventual funeral of her father-in-law, Laertes. She claimed that she would choose a husband as soon as the shroud was completed. By day, the queen, a renowned weaver, worked on a great loom in the royal halls. At night, she secretly unraveled what she had done, amazingly deceiving the young suitors. Her ploy failed only when one of her servants eventually betrayed her and told the suitors what was happening.

The contest of the bow and axes is another example of Penelope's guile; it also illustrates her wry sense of destiny. After Odysseus returns to Ithaca, the queen announces first to the visiting beggar, whom she suspects to be Odysseus, that she will hold a contest in which the suitors will be asked to string the great bow of Odysseus and shoot an arrow through a dozen axes, an old trick of her husband's, and that she will be the wife of the man who can perform the feat. The choice of this particular contest is no coincidence; Penelope knows exactly what she is doing. If the old beggar really is Odysseus in disguise, he alone has any realistic chance of winning the contest.

Telemachus

The secondary plot featuring Prince Telemachus, which scholars sometimes call the "Telemacheia," is an early example of a coming-of-age story. As the epic opens, Telemachus, about 21 years old, is on the brink of manhood, uncertain and insecure in his potential power, and in grave danger from the suitors who would prefer to see him dead.

Telemachus initially asserts himself by calling an assembly of Ithaca's leaders in order to protest the suitors' activities. Although he speaks well at the meeting and impresses some of the elders, the leading suitors

(Antinous and Eurymachus) show no respect for either Telemachus or his mother, Queen Penelope, and little is accomplished. Athena senses danger and manages for the prince to visit two foreign kings who are old comrades of his father: Nestor of Pylos and Menelaus of Sparta.

During his travels, Telemachus grows as a man. Athena, disguised as Mentor, guides and instructs him. He learns how to behave among Greek leaders. Nestor reinforces in the prince a respect for loyalty and devotion. Menelaus encourages him with news that Odysseus may be alive and held captive by a goddess-nymph named Calypso. Athena keeps the prince alive by helping him avoid an ambush set up by the suitors on his return trip to Ithaca.

After he joins his father and is made an important part of the king's plot to overcome the suitors, a good deal of Telemachus' motivation is based on faith. He believes in the support of the gods, especially Athena; and he believes in this great man, his father, whom he has known only as a legend. Telemachus rarely wavers. At the showdown with the suitors in the great hall, he is shrewd enough to get his mother out of the line of fire and mature enough to be a real help to Odysseus. The prince stands against more than a hundred suitors with only his father and a couple of herdsmen on his side. He fights valiantly, earning his father's respect and trust.

Athena (Pallas)

A daughter of Zeus and a "patron of human ingenuity" (Fables and Knox, p. 524), Athena is the one who first sent Odysseus on his wanderings as part of the punishment for a desecration of her temple by one of the Greek warriors at Troy. In *The Odyssey*, however, she is a consistent supporter of Odysseus, intervening repeatedly on behalf of the hero and his son, Telemachus.

Athena often appears in disguise, most significantly as Mentor, the family friend and adviser who instructs Telemachus in his father's absence. She is also adept at changing the appearance of humans. When Odysseus returns to Ithaca and needs a disguise in order to gather information without revealing his true identity, Athena makes him over to look like an old beggar, even wrinkling his skin and taking the fire out of his eyes (13.454–460.). When appropriate, she renews his vigor, making him look taller, stronger, and young. She breathes strength into aged Laertes and empowers him to kill Eupithes near the end of the epic.

Homer strikes a delicate balance with Athena. Her intervention is essential, but she allows the humans to earn their destinies. In the battle with the suitors, for example, she intervenes just enough to encourage Odysseus and *help* him to turn the tide; but then she recedes into the background and allows the mortals the victory.

Polyphemus (the Cyclops) and King Alcinous

The greatest contrast among the secondary characters in *The Odyssey* is between the Cyclops, that wild race of cannibalistic one-eyed giants, and the Phaeacians, the civilized, hospitable folk who encourage Odysseus to tell of his wanderings and who then sail him home to Ithaca. These are best represented by Polyphemus (sometimes simply called "the Cyclops") and King Alcinous.

The one-eyed giants are barbaric. Fortunately for them, their homeland is so lush that they need not cultivate crops. Although they are effective herdsmen, they have no interest in the usual trappings of civilization. Polyphemus and his fellow brutes have no laws, no councils, and no traditions of civility or hospitality. When Odysseus' curiosity leads him to Polyphemus' cave, his men want to raid it and leave. Odysseus insists on staying to try the hospitality of the owner, a decision that ultimately results in the death of several of his men.

A son of Poseidon and nearly as powerful as the gods, Polyphemus scoffs at the concept of hospitality and welcomes his guests by devouring two for supper. Although powerful, Polyphemus is not particularly intelligence. He is easily convinced that Odysseus' name is "Nobody," leading to confusion when Polyphemus later tells his fellow giants that Nobody is harming him. Odysseus easily gets Polyphemus drunk, blinds him, and escapes by riding underneath the rams that the blinded giant turns out to graze in the morning.

King Alcinous and his fellow Phaeacians, on the other hand, are decent, civilized, and kind. They are known for going out of their way to return a helpless stranger to his homeland. This tradition exceeds even the generous welcome that we often find in *The Odyssey* and is consistent with the Phaeacians' devotion to Zeus, protector of lost wanderers and champion of suppliants. Alcinous' people excel at seamanship and communal activities, but they are not aggressive militarily. They once lived dangerously close to the warlike Cyclops but moved to avoid trouble. Odysseus is comfortable among the Phaeacians. It is disturbing that Poseidon is allowed to punish them for their tradition of returning wayfarers to their homelands.

Circe and Calypso

The two goddesses with whom Odysseus has extended affairs are similar in that Circe is a devastatingly beautiful goddess-enchantress and Calypso is a devastatingly beautiful goddess-nymph; but they contrast in their motives toward and treatment of Odysseus. After Odysseus (following Hermes' advice) initially conquers Circe, she does everything she can to help him. In addition to releasing the spell that turned his men into swine, she is such an excellent hostess and lover to Odysseus that his men must talk him into going on with the journey a full year later. Even then, Circe helps the Greeks with supplies and advice.

Calypso, on the other hand, is an egocentric, dominating goddess who holds Odysseus captive for seven years in hopes of marrying him. When he resists and is liberated by Hermes under orders from Zeus, Calypso offers him immortality if he will stay. When he declines even that offer, Calypso leads Odysseus to believe that letting him go is her idea: "I am all compassion," she lies (5.212). While we may admire Calypso's spunk and her very early advocacy of women's sexual equality, her possessive obsessions make her more trouble than she is worth for Odysseus.

CRITICAL ESSAYS

Major Themes in *The Odyssey*

The major themes in *The Odyssey* are especially significant because they serve to form the moral and ethical constitution of most of the characters. The reader learns about the characters through the themes. The more complicated a character is, the more he or she engages these major themes. Therefore, the most complicated character, Odysseus, appropriately embodies each of the themes to one degree or another.

Hospitality

Thinking of hospitality as a major theme in a literary work may seem odd to modern readers. In Homer's world, however, hospitality is essential. Fagles and Knox (p. 45) refer to hospitality as a dominant part of "the only code of moral conduct that obtains in the insecure world of *The Odyssey*."

Arriving strangers may be dangerous or harmless, and residents are wise to be prepared for trouble. Often, however, strangers are but wayfarers, probably in need of at least some kind of help. Similarly, the residents themselves—or their friends or kin—may, at some time, be wayfarers. Civilized people, therefore, make an investment in hospitality to demonstrate their quality as human beings *and* in hopes that their own people will be treated well when they travel. Furthermore, communications are very primitive in Homer's world, and strangers bring and receive news. It was through visitors that the Homeric Greeks learned about and kept abreast of what was happening in the world beyond their local areas.

Hospitality, or the lack of it, affects Odysseus throughout the epic, and the reader can judge civility by the degree of hospitality offered. Odysseus' own home has been taken over by a horde of suitors who crudely take advantage of Ithaca's long-standing tradition of hospitality. Telemachus and Penelope lack the strength to evict them, nor can they hope for much help from the community because the suitors represent some of the strongest families in the area. In his wanderings, Odysseus receives impressive help from the Phaeacians and, initially, from Aeolus. Circe is of great assistance after Odysseus conquers her, and the Lotus-eaters might be a little *too* helpful. On the other hand, the Sirens are sweet-sounding hosts of death, and Cyclops (Polyphemus) makes no pretense toward hospitality. In fact, Polyphemus scoffs at the concept and the gods that support it.

Zeus himself, king of the gods, is known as the greatest advocate of hospitality and the suppliants who request it; yet even he allows the sea god Poseidon to punish the Phaeacians for their generous tradition of returning wayfarers to their homelands.

Loyalty

Another personal virtue that is a major theme in the epic is loyalty. The most striking example of loyalty in the epic is, of course, Penelope, who waits faithfully for 20 years for her husband's return. Another example is Telemachus, who stands by his father against the suitors. Odysseus' old nurse, Eurycleia, remains loyal to Penelope and her absent master. Eumaeus, the swineherd, and Philoetius, the cowherd, are exemplary in their loyalty to their master and his possessions. Also an excellent if humble host, Eumaeus makes his king proud as he speaks respectfully of the royal family and abhors the invasion of the suitors.

In contrast are goatherd Melanthius and maidservant Melantho. Melanthius has become friendly with the suitors and insults Odysseus while the king is still in disguise. Melantho goes even further, sleeping with the enemy, showing disrespect for the queen, and insulting the beggar/Odysseus. The loyal servants are rewarded; those who betray their master are dealt with more harshly.

This issue, however, can be complicated because many of the people from whom Odysseus expects loyalty are actually his property. Even his wife, Penelope, literally belongs to her husband. As abhorrent as that may seem to a modern reader, possession is part of the justification for a double standard when it comes to sexual fidelity. Penelope is expected to be absolutely faithful to her husband. Given the account of the battle in the hall at the end of the epic, one might well imagine what would happen to her upon Odysseus' return if she were not. Odysseus, on the other hand, is not bound by the same expectation of fidelity.

Perseverance

Penelope and Odysseus especially embody the theme of perseverance. One of the reasons that they are well matched is that they are both survivors. Odysseus has been absent for 20 years, 10 at the Trojan War and 10 more in his journey home. According to the most aggressive of the suitors, Antinous, Penelope has persevered against the invaders for about four years (2.96), playing one against another and confronting them with cunning, most notably exemplified in her ruse of weaving a shroud for her father-in-law, Laertes.

Odysseus' perseverance is legendary, especially in the section of the epic involving his wanderings (Books 9–12). Through the use of guile, courage, strength, and determination, he endures. Perhaps the most difficult test of his perseverance as well as his loyalty is the seven years he spends as Calypso's captive, a situation he can neither trick nor fight his way out. Even when the beautiful goddess-nymph tempts him with immortality, Odysseus yearns for home.

Vengeance

Poseidon and Odysseus are the most noticeable representatives of the theme of vengeance. In order to escape from the cave of the Cyclops (Polyphemus), Odysseus blinds the one-eyed giant (Book 9). Unfortunately, the Cyclops is the sea god Poseidon's son; Odysseus has engaged a formidable enemy. Poseidon can't kill Odysseus because the Fates have determined that he will make it home. However, the sea god can help to fulfill his son's wish that Odysseus should arrive in Ithaca late, broken, and alone, his shipmates lost, and his household in turmoil (9.590–95). In one of the more controversial sections of the epic, Poseidon takes his frustration out on the Phaeacians whose only offense is following their tradition of hospitality by sailing Odysseus home (13.142 ff.).

Odysseus' vengeance is formidable when it is directed toward the suitors and his disloyal servants. He demonstrates impressive tolerance as he endures, in disguise, the insults and assaults of the suitor Antinous, the goatherd Melanthius, and the maidservant Melantho, for example. Each will die a gruesome death. In a surprise attack (Book 22), Odysseus kills the suitors' leader, Antinous, first with an arrow through the throat; he then kills smooth-talking Eurymachus, the other leading suitor, with an arrow in the liver. Melanthius and Melantho die more slowly after the slaughter of the suitors. Odysseus is avenging the suitors' lack of respect for and the servants' lack of loyalty to his office, his property, and his family.

Appearance versus Reality

The theme of appearance versus reality is at the core of the relationship between Athena and Odysseus. Athena is the maven of makeovers. Her most memorable illusions in *The Odyssey* are disguises for herself or Odysseus. At the beginning of the epic, she appears to Telemachus as Mentes, king of the Taphians, an old friend of his father who has just stopped to visit in Ithaca. This allows her to encourage the prince and lead him into an expository discussion of the problems in the palace. However, she most famously appears to Telemachus as Mentor, an Ithacan adviser who helps to protect the prince from the murderous suitors and to guide him through his coming of age.

On several occasions, Athena changes Odysseus' appearance, either to disguise him or make him look even more formidable than he normally would. As Odysseus prepares for a banquet in his honor with the Phaeacians (8.20–22), for example, she alters his appearance to make him look taller, more massive, and more splendid in every way. When Odysseus returns to Ithaca in Book 13 of *The Odyssey*, Athena disguises him as an old beggar, even going so far as to shrivel his skin, remove the "russet curls" (13.456) from his head, and dim the fire in his eyes.

Of course, Odysseus is no stranger to disguise. During the Trojan War, he posed as a beggar to enter the city; he also initiated the ruse of the giant wooden horse filled with Greek soldiers, a story retold by the bard Demodocus, not realizing that the hero himself is present, during the visit to Phaeacia (8.559 ff.).

The recognition scenes with Odysseus' three family members on Ithaca provide significant and sometimes controversial twists on the theme of appearance vs. reality. He appears to his son, Telemachus, as a beggar who is visiting the family's pig farm. When they can be alone, Athena alters Odysseus' appearance to something so impressive that the prince wonders if he might not be a god. At the palace, the faithful nurse Eurycleia privately identifies Odysseus when she recognizes a scar on his leg as she bathes him; however, she vows to keep the news to herself.

Whether Penelope recognizes her husband, on the other hand, is a matter of dispute. Although at times she seems to suspect who he is, she does not officially accept him—though he wins the contest of the giant bow (Book 21) and slays the suitors (Book 22)—until he reveals his knowledge of their wedding bed. The meeting between Odysseus and his father, Laertes, (Book 24) is also somewhat controversial. Some critics argue that Odysseus, in maintaining his disguise, is needlessly cruel to the old man; others conclude that he helps to restore his father to dignity.

Athena admires Odysseus' craft and guile, saying that even a god would have to be "some champion lying cheat" (13.330) to get past him. Deception, illusion, lying and trickery often are thought to be admirable traits in *The Odyssey*. Athena enjoys them. It's easy to see why Odysseus is her favorite mortal.

Spiritual Growth

One of the questions often asked about a work of literature is whether the principal characters grow or develop as the story progresses. The theme of spiritual growth is central to *The Odyssey*, especially as it relates to Telemachus and Odysseus.

When the epic opens, Telemachus is at a loss as to how to deal with the suitors who have taken over his home and seek the hand of his mother in marriage for primarily political reasons. His own life is in danger; as a pretender to the crown, he is nothing more than so much excess baggage to the men who would be king. Telemachus needs to grow up fast. Following the usual pattern of a coming-of-age story, the youth sets out with good intentions and an admirable, if naïve, spirit. He faces various barriers, falters temporarily, but eventually prevails.

With Athena's help, Telemachus calls an assembly meeting of Ithaca's leaders and confronts the suitors. Although he speaks well, he finds very little realistic support in the community; nonetheless, he has taken the first step toward maturity.

At the suggestion of Athena, Telemachus visits two old comrades of Odysseus—King Nestor of Pylos and King Menelaus of Sparta—in hopes of learning of his father. At the courts of these great men, Telemachus learns more about himself and how a prince should comport himself than he does about Odysseus. Nevertheless, he is given some hope that his father will return. When Odysseus does come back, Telemachus survives the test of battle and earns his father's trust.

Odysseus' growth is less linear. He was already quite a man when he left for the Trojan War 20 years before. His trials have more to do with refinement of spirit; his growth is in the kind of wisdom and judgment that will make him a better king.

Early on, Odysseus feels compelled to taunt Polyphemus the Cyclops as he escapes from the one-eyed monster. Odysseus shouts his real name at the giant, making it possible for Polyphemus to identify his tormentor to Poseidon, the Cyclops' father. This brings Odysseus, and the Phaeacians, serious problems later.

When he returns to Ithaca, however, Odysseus behaves more prudently. He enters in disguise in order to obtain information about the enemy as well as knowledge of whom to trust. Even when he is taunted and assaulted by the suitors or his own servants, Odysseus manages to maintain his composure and postpone striking back. When he does strike, the time is perfect. By the end of the epic, Odysseus seems to be a wiser, more perceptive leader than he might have been had he sailed straight home from Troy.

Literary Devices of *The Odyssey*

Composed around 700 BC, *The Odyssey* is one of the earliest epics still in existence and, in many ways, sets the pattern for the genre, neatly fitting the definition of a primary epic (that is, one that grows out of oral tradition).

In *The Odyssey*, Homer employs most of the literary and poetic devices associated with epics: catalogs, digressions, long speeches, journeys or quests, various trials or tests of the hero, similes, metaphors, and divine intervention.

Elevated Language and Meter

Homer composed *The Odyssey* in a meter known as dactylic hexameter, which gives the epic its elevated style. Each line has six metrical feet. The first five feet may be made up of either dactyls and/or spondees. A dactyl is a metrical foot consisting of a long sound followed by two short sounds (BEEEEAT beat-beat). A spondee has two long sounds (BEEEEAT BEEEEAT). However a line is composed, the last metrical foot usually is a spondee (BEEEEAT BEEEEAT).

In Homer's epic poetry, composed in Ancient Greek, it is the *length* of the sound that counts, not the emphasis as is usually the case in contemporary English poetry. Translations, for obvious reasons, generally cannot mimic the metric foot of the epics and remain true to content and themes.

The Epic Simile

One of the devices used most effectively by Homer is the epic simile. A *simile* is a figure of speech in which two unlike things or concepts are shown to be similar, for poetic purposes, often through the use of the words "like" or "as." For example, we might say that a girl's hair is *like* sunshine or that her breath is rank *as* an old gym sock. An *epic simile* sometimes extends the comparison to expansive proportions. One relatively short example in *The Odyssey* appears when Odysseus and his men blind the Cyclops: "as a blacksmith plunges a glowing ax or adze / in an ice-cold bath and the metal screeches steam / and its temper hardens—that's the iron's strength— / so the eye of the Cyclops sizzled round that stake!" (9.438–41)

Seth L. Schein (*Reading the Odyssey*, 1996, pp. 15–16) neatly distinguishes between the similes of *The Iliad* and *The Odyssey*. *The Iliad* is confined geographically in ways that *The Odyssey* is not; it deals primarily with the Trojan War. *The Odyssey*, on the other hand, covers much of the known (and some of the unknown) world of the time. Because of this, Homer's similes in *The Iliad* perform two functions: First, as with most similes, they help to clarify or deepen the reader's experience of something, such as a mood, an event, an object, or thought. Second, the simile also, as Schein puts it "expand(s) the universe of the poem and the range of experience it comprehends."

In *The Odyssey*, Homer uses the epic simile differently. First, the later poem has fewer similes, and, for the most part, they do not expand the already vast world of the story. Instead, in *The Odyssey*, the similes intensify the experience for the reader. Schein and others cite the simile that Homer creates when he appropriately compares Penelope's delight, upon realizing her husband's return, to that felt by shipwrecked sailors who catch sight of shore: "Joy, warm as the joy that shipwrecked sailors feel / when they catch sight of land." (23.262–63 in Fagles). Penelope is like the shipwrecked sailors. Her life has been, in effect, lost at sea without her husband. Realizing his return is like catching sight of land.

Epithets

Homer's poetics include other noticeable devices that may seem odd to a modern reader. One is his extensive use of epithets. An *epithet* is a term or phrase used to characterize the *nature* of a character, an object, or an event. An epithet that has become a cliché because if its excessive use in earlier translations of *The Odyssey* is "rosy-fingered Dawn." Morning's first light is compared to rosy fingers spreading across the land. Fagles spares the reader slightly, while being faithful to the text, by referring to "Dawn with her rose-red fingers" (the first line of Book 2, for example).

Athena, sometimes called Pallas Athena or simply Pallas, often carries the epithet "sparkling-eyed" (1.53). Among other characteristics, hair gets a lot of attention in epithets. Circe, for example, is "the nymph with lovely braids" (10.149). Various limbs are extolled. The sea-nymph Ino is "Cadmus' daughter with lovely ankles" (5.366); the beautiful daughter of Alcinous and Arete is "[w]hite-armed Nausicaa" (6.112). In addition to identifying characters in ways that may or may not be very significant, epithets allow the poet to fill out a line and match the meter at his discretion.

Other Literary Devices

Some other literary devices, such as catalogs and digressions, may seem tedious to the modern reader. To his audience in ancient Greece, however, Homer's various lists of heroes or villains were familiar.

For modern readers, the epic also has an unusual amount of repetition. Nevertheless, this repetition is one of the features of oral tradition that help to identify *The Odyssey* as a primary epic. Repetition was used as a touchstone for the rhapsode; it helped him keep his place. Repetition aided the listener in the same way.

Major Symbols in *The Odyssey*

Homer's world in *The Odyssey* looms large, and it presents symbols, ranging from specific objects to geographical entities, that are large in their significance. Examples include the shroud that Penelope weaves for Laertes, the great bow of Odysseus, the sea itself, and the island of Ithaca.

Laertes' Shroud

The shroud that Penelope weaves for her father-in-law, Laertes', eventual funeral symbolizes the cunning with which she confronts the suitors. She lacks the power to fight them with physical strength so she wards them off with her wits. The suitor Antinous bitterly tells the story of the shroud to the assembly in Book 2: Penelope devoted herself to the shroud for three full years, promising she would choose a husband when she finished. By day, the queen, a renowned weaver, worked at a great loom in the royal halls. At night, she secretly unraveled what she had done, deceiving the young suitors. The ruse failed only when Penelope was betrayed by a disloyal maidservant.

Odysseus' Bow

Primarily, the bow symbolizes the physical superiority of the king—an important point in a world in which the mighty prevail. But the bow also symbolizes the maturity and perhaps the character of the king. The suitors can't come close to stringing it (Book 21), illustrating the fact that none of them is capable of leading Ithaca. Prince Telemachus, trying the bow just for sport, comes close. The reader is told that Telemachus probably could string the bow on his fourth attempt, but his father signals him to desist. We take from this passage that Telemachus is *almost* ready to be king but patiently and properly acquiesces to his father's judgment. Only Odysseus can string the bow on his first attempt, and he does so with ease, showing that he is the proper mate for Penelope and the only man ready to be king of Ithaca.

The Sea

The sea itself is a recurring symbol throughout the epic. It is, in effect, the sea of life. It represents a great man's journey through life with all its victories and heartbreaks.

Because Odysseus is far from Ithaca and the only way home is by way of the sea, he shows lack of judgment when he incurs the wrath of the sea god, Poseidon, by blinding the god's son Polyphemus. The sea god answers the Cyclops' prayer by making Odysseus' struggle long and hard, assuring that he returns home alone and finds formidable problems in his household. Part of the appeal of *The Odyssey* is this universal journey that we all undertake, in ways great or small.

Ithaca

The island of Ithaca symbolizes home. There Odysseus can share his life with his beloved wife and son, enjoy the wealth that he has earned, eat the food of his youth, and even sleep in the bed that he built. Ithaca symbolizes the end of the journey, the goal of the mythic trek. Nevertheless, it is not gained without a fight.

Odysseus must initially enter his own home in disguise. This is necessary because his home has been invaded by the enemy: the suitors. Being the military leader that he is, Odysseus first gathers pertinent information. He then plans the time and place of his attack, doing what he can to limit the enemy's weapons while procuring his own. His son and two loyal herdsmen stand by him, and Athena intervenes only enough to encourage victory so long as Odysseus fights well. The reward is that Odysseus resumes his proper position as king of his homeland, Ithaca.

CliffsNotes Review

Use this CliffsNotes Review to test your understanding of the original text, and reinforce what you've learned in this book. After you work through the review and essay questions, identify the quote section, and complete the fun and useful practice projects, you're well on your way to understanding a comprehensive and meaningful interpretation of *The Odyssey*.

Q&A

1. Penelope and Telemachus' home suffers from an infestation of _____.

2. Penelope delayed choosing a husband with the ruse of weaving _____.

3. The goddess-nymph Calypso holds Odysseus captive for _____ years.

4. Odysseus tells the story of his wanderings to the civilized people called _____.

5. The blinded Cyclops, Polyphemus, is the son of _____.

6. Several of Odysseus' men are turned into swine by the goddess-enchantress _____.

7. In the land of the dead, Odysseus receives advice and prophecy from the seer _____.

8. On Ithaca, Athena helps to disguise Odysseus as _____.

9. The test that Penelope schedules for Apollo's festal day involves _____.

10. Loyal old nurse Eurycleia recognizes Odysseus when she notices _____.

Answers: (1) suitors (2) a shroud for Laertes (3) seven (4) Phaeacians (5) Poseidon (6) Circe (7) Tiresias (8) an old beggar (9) stringing the great bow of Odysseus and shooting an arrow through twelve axes (10) an old scar on his leg

Identify the Quote

1. It's not the suitors here who deserve the blame, / it's your own dear mother, the matchless queen of cunning . . . . This was her latest masterpiece of guile: / she set up a great loom in the royal halls / and she began to weave . . . a shroud for old lord Laertes . . . .

2. Nobody—that's my name. Nobody.

3. There you will find them grazing, / herds and fat flocks, the cattle of Helios, / god of the sun who sees all, hears all things. / Leave the beasts unharmed . . . .

4. . . . But here he lies, / quite dead, and he incited it all—Antinous— / look, the man who drove us all to crime! . . . So spare your own people! Later we'll recoup / your costs with a tax laid down upon the land . . . .

5. Woman—your words, they cut me to the core! / Who could move my bed? Impossible task, / even for some skilled craftsman . . . . I know, I built it myself . . . .

Answers: (1) [Antinous speaks to Telemachus and the assembly in the Book 2. He rudely criticizes Penelope while actually demonstrating her cleverness and the suitors' density.] (2) [Odysseus speaks to Polyphemus in Book 9, tricking the Cyclops with a play on words.] (3) [Tiresias the prophet severely warns Odysseus in the Land of the Dead (Book 11) about eating the Sungod's cattle; Odysseus' men eventually violate the warning. When they return to the sea, Zeus kills them all as punishment.] (4) [Eurymachus, typically, tries to talk his way out of the slaughter of the suitors in Book 22, but Odysseus is having none of it and shoots an arrow into the man's liver.] (5) [Odysseus passes Penelope's final test by identifying their wedding bed.]

Essay Questions

1. The Telemachus subplot is a traditional coming-of-age story. What standard elements does this subplot share with other coming-of-age stories? Why and in what way does the prince change?

2. Consider two of the following as symbols—Odysseus' great bow, the shroud that Penelope weaves for Laertes, the island of Ithaca, or the sea itself—and explain their significance in the story.

3. How does the theme of vengeance work in the epic? Approach it from the points of view of Telemachus and Poseidon, as well as Odysseus.

4. Who is your favorite female character and why? Consider immortals as well as mortals.

5. A major theme in *The Odyssey* is reciprocity: people getting what they deserve. Explain how this theme affects the main characters: Odysseus, Penelope, Antinous, Telemachus.

6. *The Odyssey* contains certain literary devices common to primary epics. List these devices and explain their purpose. If you could change one of Homer's techniques in telling the story, what would it be? Why?

7. As an epic hero, Odysseus possesses many exemplary qualities. List and explain how they benefit him. What are his less admirable characteristics and how do these qualities cause him harm?

8. Compare and contrast the society of the Phaeacians with the lifestyle of the Cyclops and explain how these two societies represent the theme of hospitality. Then discuss the significance of hospitality to Homeric Greeks.

Practice Projects

1. Assume that Ithaca had courts of law and that the suitors were hauled into court instead of slaughtered. What would the charges be? If you represented the defense, how would you argue the case?

2. As an extensive project, read another primary epic, such as *The Iliad* or the Anglo-Saxon *Beowulf*, and compare it to *The Odyssey* in areas such as style, character, and theme.

CliffsNotes Resource Center

The learning doesn't need to stop here. CliffsNotes Resource Center shows you the best of the best—links to the best information in print and online about the author and/or related works. And don't think that this is all we've prepared for you; we've put all kinds of pertinent information at www.cliffsnotes.com. Look for all the terrific resources at your favorite bookstore or local library and on the Internet. When you're online, make your first stop www.cliffsnotes.com where you'll find more incredibly useful information about *The Odyssey.*

Books

This CliffsNotes book provides a meaningful interpretation of *The Odyssey,* published by IDG Books Worldwide, Inc. If you are looking for information about the author and/or related works, check out these other publications:

Homer's Odyssey. Harold Bloom, ed. Under the supervision of the distinguished critic and professor at Yale University, this introductory volume features selections from the critical views of scholars ranging from Aristotle (c. 335 BC) to Charles Segal in the 1990s, with a brief essay on composition, a thematic analysis, and an introduction by the editor. Broomall, PA: Chelsea House, 1996.

An Introduction to Homer, by W. A. Camps. Structure, design, and poetics are the strengths of this small volume designed primarily for the reader who is new to the epic. Short sections on background are especially helpful. Oxford: Clarendon Press, 1980.

Folk Tale, Fiction and Saga in the Homeric Epics, by Rhys Carpenter. Perhaps because the chapters originally were eight lectures presented orally, this is an unusually lucid and accessible approach to Homer, a classic study of background and composition. Berkeley: University of California Press, 1946.

The Distaff Side: Representing the Female in Homer's Odyssey. Beth Cohen, ed. This book is a must for anyone considering the female characters in the epic. With considerable emphasis on ancient Greek art, the approach is fresh and insightful. New York: Oxford University Press, 1995.

The Odyssey. Robert Fagles, trans, with introduction and notes by Bernard Knox. A superior poetic translation with readable, informative introduction and notes, the volume also contains a thorough pronouncing glossary and helpful maps. *Time* magazine called it one of the ten "Best Books of 1996." Highly recommended. New York: Penguin, 1996.

Regarding Penelope: From Character to Poetics, by Nancy Felson-Rubin. A thorough analysis of the relationship between the central human female, Penelope, and the poetics of the epic, the volume investigates her integrated roles as wife, mother, heroine, and triumphant individual. This work is extremely helpful for those studying this complex character. Princeton: Princeton University Press, 1994.

The Making of Homeric Verse: The Collected Essays of Milman Parry. Adam Parry, ed. Milman Parry's classic French and English essays on the traditional, oral, formulaic style of the epic, published originally in the late 1920s and early 1930s, are presented together here, the French translated to English, with an introduction by the editor. Oxford: Oxford University Press, 1971.

Singers, Heroes, and Gods in the Odyssey, by Charles Segal. Mythology and character are thoroughly considered in this outstanding addition to the respected Myth and Poetics series. The section on bards, liars, and beggars is especially enlightening, and no fun-loving student should miss the story about the Yukon. Ithaca: Cornell University Press, 1994.

Reading the Odyssey: Selected Interpretive Essays. Seth L. Schein, ed. Ten leading scholars present a variety of perceptive approaches to the epic, with an excellent introduction by the editor. Although some prep students will benefit from the book, it probably best suits somewhat more advanced college undergraduates or graduate scholars. Princeton: Princeton University Press, 1996.

It's easy to find books published by IDG Books Worldwide, Inc. You'll find them in your favorite bookstores (on the Internet and at a store near you). We also have three Web sites that you can use to read about all the books we publish:

- www.cliffsnotes.com
- www.dummies.com
- www.idgbooks.com

Internet

Check out these Web resources for more information about Homer and *The Odyssey*:

Ancient Greek and Hellenic Links, http://www.webcom.com/ shownet/medea/grklink.html—Selected as a "valuable Internet resource" for Discovery Channel School's *Great Books*, for *The Odyssey*, the site lists numerous links on Hellenic and Ancient Greek topics, including art, geography, literature and others.

Bulfinch's Mythology, http://www.bulfinch.org/—A great deal of information on mythology, some of which applies to Homer, including a topic search and book search.

Geocities: The Odyssey, http://www.geocities.com/Athens/ 8497/—Featuring a map of Odysseus' wanderings and an interesting photograph of the possible location of Scylla and Charybdis, the site includes a ninth-grader's impressive guide to understanding *The Odyssey.*

Greek Mythology: From the Iliad to the Fall of the Last Tyrant, http://messagenet.com/myths—This site features an introduction to Greek mythology, a comparison of Greek and Roman names, and links to other pages.

The Internet Classics Archive, http://classics.mit.edu/—Especially interested in ancient classics, the site includes contests as well as a search engine that should prove valuable for both students and teachers.

New York Times Book Archives, http://www.nytimes. com/books—This is an excellent, stable resource. The student who accesses the book section and lists a topic (author or title) should be able to find reviews, news articles, and interviews of interest.

The Odyssey-Background, http://www.mythweb.com/odyssey/ background_s.html—Features detailed background of the epic, information on characters, and an index. Cute animated graphics.

Next time you're on the Internet, don't forget to drop by www.cliffsnotes.com. We created an online Resource Center that you can use today, tomorrow, and beyond.

Films and Other Recordings

For more on *The Odyssey,* consider these films and recordings:

The Odyssey. Dir. Andrei Konchalovsky. Perf. Armand Assante and Greta Scacchi. A Hallmark Entertainment, American Zoetrope Production, 1997. Despite some impressive special effects and occasionally accurate scenes, this film version does not provide the student with a reliable account of the epic. It begins prior to the Trojan War. Several episodes and characters are distorted or cut. Three hours might be better spent reading.

Ulysses. Dir. Mario Camerini. Perf. Kirk Douglas and Anthony Quinn. A Lux Film, Ponti-De Laurentiis Production, 1955. Using the Latin name ("Ulysses") for Odysseus as its title, the film initially seems more faithful to the text than is the 1997 version. Douglas and Quinn are impressive as usual. However, the tone and special effects are dated, and many episodes are altered along the way. It is not a reliable account of the text.

The Odyssey. Fagles, Robert, trans. New York: Penguin, 1996. With introduction by Bernard Knox, contribution by Ian McKellan, nine tape cassettes. Shorter, less expensive versions are readily available; but this is an outstanding companion to the translation that *Time* magazine called one of the ten "Best Books of 1996." Fagles is faithful to the Greek in content and, remarkably, in style while creating a modern poetic translation that is lively and accessible.

Magazines and Journals:

For more information on *The Odyssey,* consider these articles:

Brown, Calvin S. "Odysseus and Polyphemus: The Name and the Curse." *Comparative Literature* 18 (1966): 193–202. Brown examines two of the central issues in Book 9 as Odysseus escapes the Cyclops.

Dimock, George. "Crime and Punishment in *The Odyssey.*" *Yale Review* 60 (1971): 199–214. For a concise consideration of criminology in the epic, this is clear and direct. Odysseus' revenge is of special interest.

Gaskin, R. "Do Homeric Heroes Make Real Decisions?" *Classical Quarterly* 40 (1990): 1–15. The decision process is investigated in the context of the epics.

Harrison, E. L. "Notes on Homeric Psychology." *Phoenix* 14 (1960): 63–80. Ancient psychology proves to be surprisingly modern.

Olson, S. D. "The Stories of Agamemnon in Homer's *Odyssey*." *Transactions of the American Philological Association* 120 (1990): 57–72. The story of Agamemnon's murder and the contrast between Clytemnestra and Penelope form a consistent backdrop throughout the epic and reflect on the themes of loyalty and vengeance.

Rutherford, R. B. "The Philosophy of the *Odyssey*." *Journal of Hellenic Studies* 106 (1986): 145–62. Students interested in a philosophical approach to the epic should find this worthwhile.

Send Us Your Favorite Tips

In your quest for knowledge, have you ever experienced that sublime moment when you figure out a trick that saves time or trouble? Perhaps you realized you were taking ten steps to accomplish something that could have taken two. Or you found a little-known workaround that achieved great results. If you've discovered a useful tip that gave you insight into or helped you understand *The Odyssey* and you'd like to share it, the CliffsNotes staff would love to hear from you. Go to our Web site at www.cliffsnotes.com and click the Talk to Us button. If we select your tip, we may publish it as part of CliffsNotes Daily, our exciting, free e-mail newsletter. To find out more or to subscribe to a newsletter, go to http://www.cliffsnotes.com on the Web.

Index

CliffsNotes

CliffsNotes

LITERATURE NOTES

Absalom, Absalom!
The Aeneid
Agamemnon
Alice in Wonderland
All the King's Men
All the Pretty Horses
All Quiet on the
    Western Front
All's Well &
    Merry Wives
American Poets of the
    20th Century
American Tragedy
Animal Farm
Anna Karenina
Anthem
Antony and Cleopatra
Aristotle's Ethics
As I Lay Dying
The Assistant
As You Like It
Atlas Shrugged
Autobiography of
    Ben Franklin
Autobiography of
    Malcolm X
The Awakening
Babbit
Bartleby & Benito
    Cereno
The Bean Trees
The Bear
The Bell Jar
Beloved
Beowulf
The Bible
Billy Budd & Typee
Black Boy
Black Like Me
Bleak House
Bless Me, Ultima
The Bluest Eye & Sula
Brave New World
Brothers Karamazov

The Call of the Wild &
    White Fang
Candide
The Canterbury Tales
Catch-22
Catcher in the Rye
The Chosen
The Color Purple
Comedy of Errors...
Connecticut Yankee
The Contender
The Count of
    Monte Cristo
Crime and Punishment
The Crucible
Cry, the Beloved
    Country
Cyrano de Bergerac
Daisy Miller &
    Turn...Screw
David Copperfield
Death of a Salesman
The Deerslayer
Diary of Anne Frank
Divine Comedy-I.
    Inferno
Divine Comedy-II.
    Purgatorio
Divine Comedy-III.
    Paradiso
Doctor Faustus
Dr. Jekyll and Mr. Hyde
Don Juan
Don Quixote
Dracula
Electra & Medea
Emerson's Essays
Emily Dickinson Poems
Emma
Ethan Frome
The Faerie Queene
Fahrenheit 451
Far from the Madding
    Crowd
A Farewell to Arms
Farewell to Manzanar
Fathers and Sons
Faulkner's Short Stories

Faust Pt. I & Pt. II
The Federalist
Flowers for Algernon
For Whom the Bell Tolls
The Fountainhead
Frankenstein
The French
    Lieutenant's Woman
The Giver
Glass Menagerie &
    Streetcar
Go Down, Moses
The Good Earth
The Grapes of Wrath
Great Expectations
The Great Gatsby
Greek Classics
Gulliver's Travels
Hamlet
The Handmaid's Tale
Hard Times
Heart of Darkness &
    Secret Sharer
Hemingway's
    Short Stories
Henry IV Part 1
Henry IV Part 2
Henry V
House Made of Dawn
The House of the
    Seven Gables
Huckleberry Finn
I Know Why the
    Caged Bird Sings
Ibsen's Plays I
Ibsen's Plays II
The Idiot
Idylls of the King
The Iliad
Incidents in the Life of
    a Slave Girl
Inherit the Wind
Invisible Man
Ivanhoe
Jane Eyre
Joseph Andrews
The Joy Luck Club
Jude the Obscure

Julius Caesar
The Jungle
Kafka's Short Stories
Keats & Shelley
The Killer Angels
King Lear
The Kitchen God's Wife
The Last of the
    Mohicans
Le Morte d'Arthur
Leaves of Grass
Les Miserables
A Lesson Before Dying
Light in August
The Light in the Forest
Lord Jim
Lord of the Flies
The Lord of the Rings
Lost Horizon
Lysistrata & Other
    Comedies
Macbeth
Madame Bovary
Main Street
The Mayor of
    Casterbridge
Measure for Measure
The Merchant
    of Venice
Middlemarch
A Midsummer Night's
    Dream
The Mill on the Floss
Moby-Dick
Moll Flanders
Mrs. Dalloway
Much Ado About
    Nothing
My Ántonia
Mythology
Narr. ...Frederick
    Douglass
Native Son
New Testament
Night
1984
Notes from the
    Underground

The Odyssey
Oedipus Trilogy
Of Human Bondage
Of Mice and Men
The Old Man and
the Sea
Old Testament
Oliver Twist
The Once and
Future King
One Day in the Life of
Ivan Denisovich
One Flew Over
Cuckoo's Nest
100 Years of Solitude
O'Neill's Plays
Othello
Our Town
The Outsiders
The Ox Bow Incident
Paradise Lost
A Passage to India
The Pearl
The Pickwick Papers
The Picture of
Dorian Gray
Pilgrim's Progress
The Plague
Plato's Euthyphro...
Plato's The Republic
Poe's Short Stories
A Portrait of the
Artist...
The Portrait of a Lady
The Power and
the Glory
Pride and Prejudice
The Prince
The Prince and
the Pauper
A Raisin in the Sun
The Red Badge of
Courage
The Red Pony
The Return of the
Native
Richard II
Richard III

The Rise of
Silas Lapham
Robinson Crusoe
Roman Classics
Romeo and Juliet
The Scarlet Letter
A Separate Peace
Shakespeare's
Comedies
Shakespeare's Histories
Shakespeare's
Minor Plays
Shakespeare's Sonnets
Shakespeare's Tragedies
Shaw's Pygmalion &
Arms...
Silas Marner
Sir Gawain...Green
Knight
Sister Carrie
Slaughterhouse-Five
Snow Falling on Cedars
Song of Solomon
Sons and Lovers
The Sound and the Fury
Steppenwolf &
Siddhartha
The Stranger
The Sun Also Rises
T.S. Eliot's Poems &
Plays
A Tale of Two Cities
The Taming of the
Shrew
Tartuffe, Misanthrope...
The Tempest
Tender Is the Night
Tess of the D'Urbervilles
Their Eyes Were
Watching God
Things Fall Apart
The Three Musketeers
To Kill a Mockingbird
Tom Jones
Tom Sawyer
Treasure Island &
Kidnapped
The Trial

Tristram Shandy
Troilus and Cressida
Twelfth Night
Ulysses
Uncle Tom's Cabin
The Unvanquished
Utopia
Vanity Fair
Vonnegut's Works
Waiting for Godot
Walden
Walden Two
War and Peace
Who's Afraid of
Virginia...
Winesburg, Ohio
The Winter's Tale
The Woman Warrior
Worldly Philosophers
Wuthering Heights
A Yellow Raft in
Blue Water

Check Out the All-New CliffsNotes Guides

TECHNOLOGY TOPICS
Balancing Your Check-
book with Quicken
Buying and Selling
on eBay
Buying Your First PC
Creating a Winning
PowerPoint 2000
Presentation
Creating Web Pages
with HTML
Creating Your First
Web Page
Exploring the World
with Yahoo!
Getting on the Internet
Going Online with AOL
Making Windows 98
Work for You

Setting Up a
Windows 98
Home Network
Shopping Online Safely
Upgrading and
Repairing Your PC
Using Your First iMac
Using Your First PC
Writing Your First
Computer Program

PERSONAL FINANCE TOPICS
Budgeting & Saving
Your Money
Getting a Loan
Getting Out of Debt
Investing for the
First Time
Investing in
401(k) Plans
Investing in IRAs
Investing in
Mutual Funds
Investing in the
Stock Market
Managing Your Money
Planning Your
Retirement
Understanding
Health Insurance
Understanding
Life Insurance

CAREER TOPICS
Delivering a Winning
Job Interview
Finding a Job
on the Web
Getting a Job
Writing a Great Resume